WATERLOO LOCAL
MIDDLE SCHOOL L
TITLE IV B

7963
BUT

The Willie Horton Story

Books by Hal Butler

BASEBALL ALL STAR GAME THRILLS

THE BOB ALLISON STORY

THE HARMON KILLEBREW STORY

ROAR OF THE ROAD
 The Story of Auto Racing

STORMIN' NORMAN CASH

THERE'S NOTHING NEW IN SPORTS
 The Story of How Sports Began

UNDERDOGS OF SPORT

THE WILLIE HORTON STORY

The Willie Horton Story

by HAL BUTLER

JULIAN MESSNER NEW YORK

Published in the United States by
Julian Messner, a division of Simon & Schuster, Inc.,
1 West 39 Street, New York, N.Y. 10018. All rights reserved.

Copyright, ©, 1970 by Hal Butler

Second Printing, 1972

Printed in the United States of America

ISBN 0–671–32333–4 Cloth Trade
ISBN 0–671–32334–2 MCE

Library of Congress Catalog Card No. 72-123171

The Willie Horton Story

Stars of the outfield and the infield—Willie Horton, left field and Dick McAuliffe, second base, watching the Tigers at practice game.

Willie Horton's mighty swing has made him one of the most feared sluggers of the American League.

Willie never did like sliding pads inside his uniform. Reason: he's not very fast, seldom steals bases so he rarely has to slide. Here he is snipping the pads out of his uniform.

Willie Horton was voted the Most Exciting Player of the Year by the Detroit Baseball Writers in 1965. At the banquet on his left is Charlie Dressen, then manager of the Tigers and the man who acted as a second father to Willie; on the right is Jim Campbell, general manager of the Detroit Tigers.

Chapter 1

The four softball teams from Franklin School in Detroit had completed their Saturday morning games. Now the boys sat inside the gym patiently awaiting the arrival of Willie Horton, star left fielder of the Detroit Tigers. Joe Falls, sports editor of the *Detroit Free Press*, who had arranged the meeting between Horton and the boys, looked at his wristwatch. It was exactly 11:00 A.M. and Horton was due to arrive at any moment.

"You think he'll show up?" one of the boys asked.

Another shrugged. "I bet he won't. Why should he waste his time on a bunch of kids like us?"

"He'll be here," said a third boy stoutly. "Willie Horton's a good guy."

Falls threw a glance at the chattering boys and smiled. They were fidgety, shifting their positions and squirming, each of them concerned because Willie Horton had not yet arrived. But Falls knew the third boy was right. Horton was, indeed, a "good guy," and there wasn't much doubt that he would put in an appearance.

Falls walked outside and stood waiting for several minutes. Finally a big powder-blue Cadillac rolled into the schoolyard and stopped near the gym door. Willie Horton, twenty-six-year-old Negro star, detached his five-foot-ten-inch, 195-pound frame from the driver's seat, slammed shut the door of the car and looked around with a concerned expression on his face.

"Hi, Willie," Falls greeted.

"Hi, Joe." Horton kept looking around. "Didn't the boys wait for me?"

Falls grinned. It was typical of Horton to be concerned about his meeting with the youngsters. What he apparently did not realize was that the boys would have waited until Christmas for his appearance.

"They're inside," Falls said, and led Willie to the gym door.

Applause and boyish cheering rang out as Horton came through the door. Falls introduced him and Horton took his place in front of the boys.

"You fellas scared me," he said. "I thought you'd all gone home."

Then Willie began to talk. He spoke only a little about baseball and the Detroit Tigers, but he impressed the youngsters mightily with what he did say.

"When I was your age," he told them, "I used to get out of school in the afternoon and have nothing to do but hang around on street corners. I know how lonely that is. I know how you can get into trouble doing that. It's just no good to stand around doing nothing, having nothing on your mind."

He looked them over carefully. "The reason I know all this is because I had the same problems you have. I know what you do and how you think. You stand around and you get bored and the first thing you know you're punching at each other and then there's a real fight. So why do you want to fight? It won't get you anywhere. You have an argument to settle, why not get a ball and bat and settle it on the ball field? Or if you don't like baseball, beat each other some other way—in a game."

He softened his hard advice with a broad smile. "I know another thing. You kids want to smoke, don't you? Why? It won't do you any good, either. It'll ruin your health. What you've got to do is use the time you have on something that will help you."

The boys were quiet, listening intently. They were white, black and Mexican, but neither color nor nationality mattered at the moment. They were listening to Willie Horton, star left fielder of the Detroit Tigers.

"You want to know what to do with your time?" Horton went on. "I'll tell you. Everybody has to have a challenge in their lives, and it's up to each of you to find something that will give you that challenge. Something you want to do more than anything in life. For me that was baseball, but for you it might be something else. It could be singing or painting. Maybe you want to be a doctor or lawyer or a good mechanic. It doesn't matter what it is—you just have to find it for yourself and make it your life."

The boys were spellbound. They listened as Willie told how much baseball had meant to him. "It's done everything for me. It's allowed me to help my folks to move out of a bad neighborhood and into a good place so they were able to live nice for a few years. It's helped me to do the same. I guess you can say, too, that baseball made a man out of me."

Willie Horton talked for about twenty minutes. The boys were hushed, and the squirming on the hardwood floor stopped as they looked with admiration at the star outfielder who had come up from Detroit's ghetto to make himself one of the most popular and honored men in the city. And when he had finished and signed autographs for them, they went home thinking of what this man had become, all because of his dedication to one important thing in his life—baseball.

The big left fielder's message had been impressive. It had been impressive because it came from a man who knew what he was talking about.

Willie Horton had known poverty, and the loneliness and bitterness that go with it.

William Wattison Horton was born on October 18, 1942, in the coal mining town of Arno, Virginia. He was the youngest of twenty-one children—thirteen girls and eight boys—born to Clinton and Lillian Horton, and the only one to become a ballplayer.

Willie's father was a coal miner who spent long, dirty hours in black corridors drilled into the Virginia earth. When he came out of the mines at the end of a long day's work, his face was smeared with coal dust and every bone in his body ached, but he was a welcome sight to young Willie when he strode up to the ramshackle frame house that was the family home. Willie would run out to meet him, hoping that in his father's lunch pail there might be a leftover cookie or other treat for him.

Usually there was—but not always. Life was hard for the huge Horton family. Stretching a coal miner's wages far enough to buy food, clothing and shelter for twenty-one children was almost an act of magic. There were hungry days, and cold days, and days of despair. Seven of the children died at an early age.

Willie was eight years old when his father retired from mining and moved his family to Detroit. Clinton Horton felt that he was now too old to descend into the mine each day, and Detroit seemed like a thriving city where other, maybe better employment could be obtained. He moved his family—now reduced to five since all the sons and daughters except three were married—into a small two-room apartment on West Forest Avenue in the heart of the Negro district and set out to find work. It was then that his dreams crashed around him.

He found to his dismay that his skills as a coal miner were of little value in Detroit. Besides, he was too old. He walked the streets for long hours, looking for work—any kind of work—and many times he came home completely frustrated. And life in Detroit, far from being an improvement, became even harder than it had been in Arno.

The apartment in which the Horton family huddled was barely large enough to accommodate them. Their two rooms were jammed with beds, and they had to share bathroom and kitchen facilities with another family. There was often little or no food on the table. Willie's father picked up odd jobs wherever he could, and his mother put aside her job of raising the family to take in ironing or collect milk bottles for the deposit money she could get. Willie, now attending Hancock grade school and going into the first year of his teens, was becoming more aware of the family plight. And seeking to escape from the stifling environment of the dingy apartment, young Willie took to the streets.

That spelled trouble. Willie was never actually arrested and never got into serious difficulty, but boyhood pranks got him warned by the police on several occasions. He was in an environment and a situation where he might have become involved in real trouble if it had not been for one thing. It was at this critical time in his life that he was introduced to baseball.

At the age of thirteen Willie enjoyed his first experience in organized baseball—with a softball team. He found at once that baseball was a game that intrigued him and one for which he apparently had a natural talent. Willie was big for his age, and his developing muscles were large enough to permit him to hit a ball farther than most youngsters his age.

But *real* baseball, in Willie's estimation, was not the softball variety, and the following year he joined a team in the Billy Rogell Little League, sponsored by ex-Tiger shortstop Rogell himself. His large size and good throwing arm won him a job as catcher.

Young Willie Horton didn't know it at the time, but it was at this tender age of fourteen that Detroit Tiger scout Lou D'Annunzio got his first glimpse of him. Obviously, Willie was much too young to sign a contract with the Tigers or even with a minor league club, but D'Annunzio mentioned his name in the Tiger front office and promised to keep an eye on him as he developed.

"Even now he does everything well," D'Annunzio told the Tiger brass. "He has a natural swing and a lot of strength. But most important of all, he has a desire to improve."

The Tigers at the time were reluctant to sign Negro ballplayers and one of the officials asked, "What race is he?"

D'Annunzio couldn't see much sense to that question and, with a perfectly straight face, said, "I don't know. The next time I see him, I'll look."

Although Willie Horton loved baseball, he was not giving all of his time to the game. He was still searching for his place in life, and at one point he considered a career in boxing. Since he was a big fellow and looked older than he was, he lied about his age and worked his way into both the Golden Gloves and CYO boxing tournaments. Knowing his parents would not appreciate his efforts in boxing, he did not tell them he had entered the tournaments.

One night he came home with a bruised face and his parents looked at him with concern.

"What happened to you, Willie?" his mother asked.

Willie looked down at his shoes. "I'm sorry, Mom. I got in a street fight."

But Willie found that lies catch up with you. One night he was fighting in a tournament and the action was televised by a station in Windsor, the Canadian city across the river from Detroit. It so happened that his father saw the telecast—and there was his boy Willie in the ring. When Willie got home that night the boom was lowered.

"No more fighting!" was the word from his father, and thereafter young Willie Horton put aside the boxing gloves for a catcher's mitt and concentrated on baseball.

It was a good thing for baseball that he did, for Willie Horton rose rapidly from the lowest class of amateur baseball to the major leagues. In 1958, when he was not yet sixteen years of age, Willie joined the Class E Ravens, a Detroit sandlot team representing Walway's Standard Gas Station, as a catcher. In those days the ball field at Northwestern High School was the hotbed of sandlot baseball in Detroit. Scouts from most major league teams haunted the area, and Willie impressed quite a number of them even in his first year of sandlot play. But he was still too young to sign, and the scouts bided their time as they watched his talent grow. When Willie batted .470 for Walway's the following year, it raised a few eyebrows among those interested in young prospects.

In the same year that he started playing sandlot ball, Willie Horton enrolled at Northwestern High School. At once he went out for baseball and football. Sam Bishop, the athletic director at Northwestern, immediately saw the talent that young Willie had for baseball.

"I'd advise you to give up football and concentrate on baseball," Bishop told him bluntly.

"Why?" Willie wanted to know. "Can't I play both?"

"You *can* play both," Bishop admitted, "but your talent is obviously in baseball. In football you probably wouldn't go far, in baseball—well, the sky could be the limit."

"Yeah, but—"

"Look, Willie. I'm speaking from experience. I lost a job in the major leagues because I broke a shoulder playing football. I might have been a big league baseball player if it hadn't been for that."

"Well, Mr. Bishop, I sure would like to be a big league ballplayer," Willie admitted.

"Then stick with it and concentrate on it," said Bishop.

It was good advice, and the first advice given to him by Sam Bishop, who was later to become an important man in Willie's baseball career.

From the beginning there was never any doubt in Bishop's mind about Willie Horton's ability. The only thing in question was where he would best fit in the high school lineup. Since Bishop needed a shortstop at the time, he decided to try Willie at that position. It was almost a disaster—for the other infielders.

Willie handled the position well. The only difficulty was that he threw too hard. The first baseman and other infielders taking his throws, often at short range, complained that the ball almost tore off their gloves. Bishop shook his head sadly.

"Someday he'll kill somebody with one of those throws," he decided, and put him back of the plate as a catcher. "Most of his throws from there will be diagonally across the diamond to second base," Bishop reasoned. "That's safer."

Willie developed rapidly as a catcher; and with his lusty hitting, Northwestern High became a feared team in the Public School League. In 1959 Northwestern had an excellent team and at the finish they found themselves in line to play Cass Technical High for the Detroit Public School League high school championship. The game was to be held at Tiger Stadium (then called Briggs Stadium). Willie was thrilled at the prospect of playing ball in a major league park.

"My folks will be there to watch," he said. "I just hope I do well."

He did very well indeed, for it was in that game that Willie Horton, still a fledgling sixteen-year old, performed a feat that sent major league scouts scurrying to telephones with glowing news of "a great big Negro kid that's going to become an outstanding major leaguer."

Chapter 2

There were plenty of big league scouts in the stands when Northwestern High and Cass Tech clashed for the city championship on that warm day in June. And what they saw was mostly lusty hitting, for the game ended with Northwestern downing Cass Tech by a 13–10 score. But of all the hitting that was done that day, none was more impressive than the single blow delivered by the sixteen-year-old Willie Horton.

Halfway through the game he strode to the plate and carefully set himself in the right-hand batter's box. On the mound for Cass Tech was a boy named George Cojocari. Cojocari got behind 2–0 on the count and had to come in with one—and Willie swung at it. The ball took off like a rocket, climbing high and far and finally crashing into the upper-deck stands in deep right field for a home run.

It was a tremendous blow for a right-hander, since it was hit to the *wrong* field for a right-handed batter and traveled a good 400 feet. And it was hit by a boy who had not yet reached his full growth and strength!

For a moment the scouts in the stands were stunned. Pat

Mullin, a Tiger scout who had once played for Detroit, shook his head in dismay.

"I never in my life saw a sixteen-year-old hit a ball that far," he said. Then he went out into the empty right field stands, retrieved the ball, and presented it to Horton after the game.

Horton's face was split with a grin in the clubhouse.

"That was quite a poke," Mullin said.

"Yeah," admitted Willie truthfully. "It sure felt good."

"Who was pitching?" a reporter asked.

Willie looked puzzled. He rarely remembered names or statistics, and he shrugged his shoulders helplessly.

"I don't think I ever got the kid's name," he said.

It was a heady moment and Willie enjoyed it. But it did not completely erase the fact that many of Horton's high school days were tempered with sadness. The Horton family was so poor that Willie had to wear old and patched clothing to school. This would have been no problem for Willie had it not been for thoughtless schoolmates who teased him about the way he looked. Finally, disgusted with the treatment he was receiving and anxious to help the family over its financial hurdle, Willie decided to drop out of school. When Sam Bishop heard of his intentions, he took Willie aside.

"Look, young man," he said. "I know your family's situation and I know you want to help them. And I know you can drop out of school if you have a good excuse. But, Willie, whatever you do, *don't* drop out!"

"But, Mr. Bishop—I could go to work to help the family and still keep up my baseball career by playing sandlot ball on weekends and—"

"Willie, listen to me," said Bishop. "Suppose you drop out and get a job in a factory and you don't make it in baseball. What of the future? You'll never be anything better than a factory worker. Let me tell you about my experience. I dropped out of school when I was thirteen, and I went to work. I worked in a factory for ten years before I saw the light. You know what I did? I went back to school. I was twenty-three years old and I was in the tenth grade, but I got my education and I went on to become an athletic coach. So the thing is, get your education now, while you're young. You'll be making a big mistake if you drop out."

What Bishop said made sense, and Willie began to reconsider. To help him come to the right conclusion, Sam Bishop bought Willie clothing and shoes out of his own pocket so that he could stay in high school. Willie was so overwhelmed by the kindness that he was almost in tears.

"I don't know how to thank you," he mumbled. "I guess I just have to stay in school now."

"You'll never regret it," Bishop said.

Willie never did. In fact, he found that his talents as a ballplayer, as well as his new clothes, made him a big man on campus. Everyone suddenly wanted to be Willie's friend, to know him and be with him. But there was one young lady in school who knew nothing at all about him. She was a reporter on Northwestern's high school paper, and one day the editor asked her to interview Willie Horton.

"Who's Willie Horton?" she asked.

"You mean you never heard of him?"

"No."

"Maybe," said the editor dubiously, "we'd better give the assignment to somebody else."

The reporter was Patricia Strickland, and several months later she met Willie Horton at a high school prom. She was the girl who, in a couple of years, would become Mrs. Willie Horton.

Willie's baseball career continued to boom. He played high school and sandlot ball simultaneously, and he was a standout catcher in both. By 1960 he was playing Class D ball on the sandlots for a team co-sponsored by Walway's Standard Gas Station and Brown Insulation. He did so well in Class D that he was selected by the Lundquist Insurance team as an added player for the Class D National Baseball Federation Tournament to be held in Altoona, Pennsylvania. With him was another young Detroit sandlotter who was to become a name in baseball—Bill Freehan.

Willie was thrilled at the prospect of playing in the tournament.

"Wish me luck," he told his father.

The elder Horton grinned broadly. "You'll do fine, Willie," he said. "I know you will." By this time Willie's father could see quite plainly the talent that was developing in his youngest son, and he was encouraging him to continue to play ball at every opportunity.

"It's where your future lies," he said.

The day before the big trip to Altoona, Lou D'Annunzio, the Tiger scout who was in charge of the team, warned the players to be on time. The bus to Altoona was to leave at 10:00 A.M. sharp.

That night Willie went to bed early. "I've got to get up early tomorrow," he explained, "to catch the bus to Altoona."

Willie took no chances. Early, to him, was five o'clock in the morning. When he arrived at the meeting place, dawn was just starting to streak the sky and the place was deserted. Willie walked to a park bench, pillowed his head on his catcher's mitt, and went to sleep.

D'Annunzio arrived almost two hours earlier than scheduled and to his amazement saw Willie lying on the bench. He walked over and woke him.

"What are you doing here so early?" he demanded.

Horton sat up sleepily, rubbing his eyes. "I didn't want to miss the bus, Mr. D'Annunzio," he said simply.

"But the bus doesn't leave until ten," D'Annunzio said.

"I know it."

D'Annunzio studied Willie keenly. "What time did you get here, anyway?" he asked.

"Oh, six o'clock, I guess." Horton looked at his shoes sheepishly. "I didn't want to miss the bus," he said again.

D'Annunzio smiled. He said nothing more. He knew Horton's fantastic high school and sandlot record, what a fine player he was and what power he had in his muscular arms. Now he knew something else. Willie Horton was completely dedicated to the game of baseball. Showing up at six o'clock to make a ten o'clock bus was proof of it.

The tournament lasted six games, and Horton batted .600 in the series. He was an important factor in bringing the tournament championship to Lundquist Insurance, but when the Most Valuable Player Award was presented after the tourney was over, Bill Freehan received it.

"I don't really deserve this," he said in his acceptance speech. "It should go to Willie Horton."

It was about this same time that an amateur all-star sandlot game was played at Briggs Stadium. Both Horton and Freehan were members of the team. Ed Katalinas, a Tiger scout, was in charge of the game. When it was over, Horton approached Katalinas.

"Is it okay if Bill and me hit a few more?" he asked.

"Batting practice?" Katalinas asked.

"Yeah. We'd just like to hit a few more."

"All right," Katalinas said, and then stepped back to watch the two powerfully built boys go at it.

What developed was a home run derby. Freehan batted first and walloped two drives into the left field seats. Then Horton stepped into the batter's box and laced two of his own into the stands. Freehand went up and hit another, and Horton duplicated it.

On the sidelines Katalinas scratched his chin thoughtfully. A home run hitting contest—and both of them staying even in the count.

When they had each hit a half dozen balls into the stands, Katalinas called a halt.

"That'll be all for today, boys," he said.

"Can't we just hit one more round?" asked Horton eagerly.

"Uh-uh. Back to the clubhouse."

Ed Katalinas was smiling as the two walked to the dugout together. Both of these boys had talent, and it wouldn't be long now before they would be signing major league contracts.

Katalinas wasn't the only scout who felt that way—especially about Horton. By the time Willie approached his graduation from high school, almost every club in both major leagues had talked to him. Four of them were actively interested in the big high school slugger: the Detroit Tigers, Minnesota Twins, New York Yankees and Boston Red Sox. Knowing that one of the clubs would soon make an offer, Sam Bishop talked to Willie's parents and decided to retain Damon Keith, a former graduate of Northwestern High and a lawyer, to handle the financial arrangements.

"That's fine with me," Willie agreed. "I'd rather somebody else did all that negotiating."

Bishop called Keith. "I've got an unusual boy here," he said. "He isn't much with the books, but he has the makings of a fine ballplayer. I wish you'd come out and take a look at him."

Keith did so and was immediately impressed. After a visit with the Horton family, Keith was made legal guardian for the under-age Willie. And when Willie graduated from Northwestern High, the offers began coming in—from Boston, New York, Minnesota.

But the offers were usually tempered with some doubt. Rumors had gotten around that Willie had a propensity for getting into trouble, that as a boy he had been watched closely by the police.

Some of the teams were afraid they would have a problem player on their hands. Scout Maurice DeLoof, of the Red Sox, made a strong bid, and when Keith told him that some others had gone higher, he shied away.

The Tigers' D'Annunzio, however, had no fears. "I'll stake my reputation on Willie's character," he told the Tiger brass. "Some people say Willie is a bad boy. I know he isn't. I know what he's got inside of him, what he's got in his heart, and that's what counts."

And so it was that on August 7, 1961, in the office of Tiger general manager James A. Campbell, Damon Keith negotiated and signed in behalf of the eighteen-year old Willie Horton a contract calling for $50,000 in bonus and salary. Of the amount —more money than Willie had ever dreamed of—he received $13,000 immediately. It was arranged for Keith, as legal guardian, to handle the rest of the money, making wise investments for Willie and doling it out to him as he needed it.

But the most poignant moment came when Willie Horton got his hands on the $13,000 advance payment. Immediately his mind raced back to the tiny apartment on West Forest Avenue, the bare table at dinnertime and the bitter plight of his mother and father.

"With this money," he told Keith, "I want to buy a home for my parents."

Chapter 3

From the time of signing his contract Willie Horton was a busy young man. He went to Grand Rapids, Michigan, and joined a team called the Sullivans to finish out the summer season. The Tigers were interested in making Horton into an outfielder, and Willie played right, left and center for the Sullivans. When the Sullivans traveled to Wichita, Kansas, to play a doubleheader with a collection of all-stars, Willie went along—his first "road trip" with a baseball team. Not only that, he stole the show by getting four hits in seven times up, leading the Sullivans to a split of the twin bill.

Along with all of this activity, Willie found time to move the Horton family to a nice ten-room home on Edison Avenue in north-central Detroit—which Willie proudly called "out in the suburbs." And with a sizable amount to support him, Willie took another important step in his young life—he married attractive Patricia Strickland, his high school sweetheart, on December 18, 1961.

When winter began to close in on the Detroit area, Willie and his wife left for Florida, where Patricia got acquainted with the warmth of the southland and Willie played baseball for the Tigers' entry in the Florida Winter League at Tampa. This course of events had been recommended by Tiger management as a prelude to Willie's first appearance at the Tiger spring training camp at Lakeland in March.

However, Horton didn't report to the main Tiger camp at Lakeland that spring, but to the rookie base called Tigertown. He was one of many rookies being tried out by the Tigers, and there were some wise baseball men looking him over and appraising him. Willie played mostly in the outfield and did reasonably well.

"He's a diamond in the rough," was the opinion expressed by most of the Tiger brass. "He needs some of the rough edges knocked off. But he's going to be a good one."

Obviously, it was not in the cards for the Tigers to keep Willie Horton on the parent club in 1962. They had him slated for an eventual outfield berth with the Tigers, but there was a lot of emphasis on the word "eventual." After all, the Tigers had a strong trio in their outfield that wasn't about to be broken up for a nineteen-year-old rookie. The trio consisted of Al Kaline, Billy Bruton and Rocky Colavito.

So when cutdown time came, Willie Horton was assigned to play for Duluth-Superior in the Class C Northern League. He took the assignment philosophically.

"I didn't really expect to stay with the Tigers this year," he told Patricia, "and a full year of play up in Duluth will do me a lot of good."

"It won't be long," Patricia said with wifely confidence, "before you'll be playing with the Tigers."

Willie smiled. Playing with the Tigers! It had been a big dream for a long time and maybe—just maybe—it was going to happen!

When Horton reported to the Duluth-Superior Dukes, he was

greeted by manager Al Lakeland. Lakeland surveyed Willie's muscular arms and body.

"We need a hard-hitting outfielder," he said. "I think you can help this club."

"I hope so," said Horton.

"You'll play regularly up here," Lakeland said, "and that'll be good for you."

As it turned out, it was good for the Dukes too. Willie Horton had a highly successful season with Duluth-Superior. He played in 123 games and posted a neat batting average of .295. Among his 130 hits were 20 doubles, 4 triples and 15 homers. He also batted in 72 runs, and his fielding average was .949.

When the Duluth-Superior season ended, Willie and his wife returned to Detroit. But baseball didn't end with the season for Willie. Dedicated to improving himself, he spent hours in the basement of his home swinging a bat.

"You have to develop a smooth swing," he said. "And the only way you can do it is to practice."

Willie had agreed to play winter ball at Dunedin in the Florida Instructional League, and early in the fall he left for the south—along with two other Tigers-to-be from the Duluth-Superior Dukes, Mickey Stanley and Jim Northrup. Patricia, who was now awaiting a child, stayed in Detroit.

It was on October 10, 1962, that Willie Horton received word in Florida that Patricia had given birth to a boy. The baby was named Darryl William Horton. Willie was all smiles, but he was awed too.

"Imagine me, a father!" he said. "Man, I can't hardly believe it!"

Willie enjoyed a good winter season in Florida, and when it came time to report for spring training he was called up to the main Tiger camp in Lakeland. Bob Scheffing, the sandy-haired, amiable manager of the Tigers, found himself watching Willie's performance—especially in the batters' box—with a great deal of interest. A full season at Duluth and two seasons of winter ball had done things to Willie Horton. His swing was smoother, he was fooled less often by pitchers, and—most beautiful of all in the eyes of Scheffing—he had the ability and strength to hit a ball a long way.

"He's a year or two away," thought Scheffing, "but he'll be with this club soon, and for a long time."

Indicative of things to come was an afternoon at Lakeland when a team composed of Tiger farm hands, including Horton, faced Minoru Murayama, the pitching ace of the Hanshin Tigers of Japan, in an exhibition game. Tiger general manager Jim Campbell was sitting in the stands with a couple of writers watching the contest, and when Willie Horton stepped up to the plate, Campbell filled the writers in with a little information.

"We expect this kid to develop into a good power hitter," he said, pointing toward Horton. "He hit fifteen home runs for Duluth-Superior last year, his first year out. Take a good look at him."

It was at that precise moment that Willie Horton swung at one of Murayama's tricky slants and drove the ball against the left center field wall for a long double.

"You see what I mean?" grinned Campbell.

Despite such heroics as this, Horton was fated to serve another year in the minor leagues in 1963. What made his chances of sticking with the Tigers so slim was the same thing that had made it impossible the year before. The Tigers still had Kaline, Bruton and Colavito in their outfield—three stars with no intention of giving up their jobs.

Horton had appraised the situation realistically. "Naturally," he had said when he first reported, "I'll try hard to make the big club, but if I miss I won't be disappointed. I'm pretty sure I'll land with one of the big minor league teams like Syracuse or Knoxville."

As it turned out, Willie was right. He landed with both of them in 1963.

General manager Jim Campbell and Charlie Dressen, who had taken over the field manager's job from Bob Scheffing midway in the 1962 season, were both high on Willie Horton. Both looked forward to the day when he would blossom out as a full-blown star. But both agreed that that day was not to be in 1963, and that Willie needed more experience to make him a real major leaguer.

"Let's try him at Syracuse," suggested Campbell.

"Triple A?"

"Sure. I think he can make the jump."

It was quite a jump to expect Horton to make. He would be going from Class C to Triple A ball in one season, which meant that he would be facing tougher pitching than he ever had before. The thought worried him.

"I'll just have to do the best I can," he said to his wife. "You play this game the best you know how, and you hope that it's good enough."

Willie Horton reported to the Syracuse Chiefs in the International League and was greeted by manager Bob Swift. Swift was an ex-Tiger catcher and a wise baseball man.

"This is a fast league," he said to Horton, "but we think you can make it here."

Willie nodded. He would have to make it, he thought, because if you didn't make it here you were a dead duck as far as moving up to the majors was concerned.

The Syracuse Chiefs opened their season against Atlanta, and Willie developed a serious case of butterflies in the stomach just before the game. He went back into the clubhouse and sat down for a moment. The clubhouse was empty, silent, lonely. He sat for a while, thinking, looking down at his feet, at his big hands that would soon be grasping a bat as he took his place in the batter's box against this fearful Triple A pitching.

Suddenly he was aware of another man close by, and when he looked up he saw it was Bob Swift.

"What's the matter, Willie?" asked Swift.

Horton hesitated. He shuffled his feet. "Oh, nothing," he said.

Swift looked at him suspiciously. "Then what are you doing in here?" he demanded.

"Nothing. Just thinking, I guess."

"Something must be wrong," said Swift flatly. "What is it?"

"It's nothing."

"Come on, out with it!"

Horton shuffled his feet again. Then he looked up sheepishly. "Mr. Swift," he said slowly, "what do you do for sweating hands?"

Swift smiled at the nervous Horton. "I guess the only thing you can do," he said, "is quit standing there thinking about it and go out there and play baseball."

Horton stood up. He grinned. "I guess you're right," he said, and ambled through the runway to the field.

Horton tried to put aside his worries and play baseball, but it didn't work. He found Triple A pitching completely baffling. He was tight, trying too hard, pressing. He played in 21 games for Syracuse, was at bat 78 times and got 17 hits for a meager batting average of .218. At last Swift called Horton into his office.

"Willie, we've decided to send you down to Knoxville," he said "That's Class A and they play a good brand of ball down there. We think it might get you started."

It was a blow to Horton's morale to be kicked down to Knoxville, but he could see the wisdom of it. "I hope it gets me started," he said solemnly. "I know I haven't been doing too well up here."

"Just try to stay loose down there," advised Swift. "Quit worrying. You've got ability or you wouldn't have come this far."

Horton called his parents in Detroit and told them what had happened. His father, who was a continual source of encouragement to him, said, "I wouldn't worry about it. It will probably help you to play Class A ball. I don't have any doubt that you're going to make it to the Tigers soon."

So Willie traveled with his wife and small child to Knoxville in the Class A Sally League, where he was greeted by manager Frank Carswell.

"We'll get you straightened around," Carswell said with confidence. "You've got muscles on your muscles and you'll be knocking that ball clear out of the state of Tennessee before long."

But Carswell's prediction didn't come true—at least, not at first. Willie Horton discovered right away that he couldn't hit Class A pitching either. He found himself in a discouraging slump, and in his first forty times at bat he got only three hits.

Willie began to feel that his world was slipping away from him, that all his big dreams were fading, that maybe he wasn't going to make it in baseball after all. It was at this low moment in Willie's career that a groundskeeper for the Knoxville Smokies approached him.

"I've got a good luck charm for you, Willie," he said.

In his hand he held a chestnut. Willie took it and looked at it dubiously.

"It'll bring you luck, Willie," the groundskeeper insisted.

Horton put it in his pocket. "Thanks," he said. "I sure hope it brings me luck. I hope things start opening up for me."

Chapter 4

There might have been something to the psychology of having a lucky chestnut in his pocket, but more likely it was the fact that things just "started to open up" for Willie. Because from that time on he became a ballplayer. He hit well and played his position in left field flawlessly. Before the season was over he was voted to the Sally League All-Star team and represented the Knoxville Smokies in the annual game at Augusta, Georgia. When the figures were all in at the end of the Sally League season in September, Willie's record was a good one. He had played in 118 games, batted a fine .333, and driven in 70 runs. Among his 147 hits were 14 home runs, 9 triples and 20 doubles. His .333 batting average missed the Sally League batting title by only four points.

These impressive figures didn't go unnoticed in the Tiger front office. The Tigers were in a battle for fourth place in the American League at the time, and there was some thought that Willie Horton's power might just come in handy at the tail end of the season.

So Willie Horton was called up by the Tigers for the last fifteen games of the season and the experience shook him.

"The Tigers!" he said in surprise. "Man, I hope I can help them a little. I hope I can do something they'll notice. Just anything at all!"

Willie Horton joined the Tigers on September 10 in Washington, D.C., where Detroit was playing the Senators in a doubleheader. The new, bowl-shaped D.C. Stadium was an impressive sight to Willie as he debarked from a taxicab and stared up at its ramparts. From the sounds of the crowd within, Horton knew that the first game had already started. He quickly found the Tiger clubhouse, and the clubhouse attendant presented him with a Tiger uniform.

The locker room was as silent as a tomb, for the Tigers were all on the field. Horton looked at the uniform, with the big "D" emblazoned on the front of the shirt and the number 23 on the back. He got suited up quickly, took a deep breath to fortify himself and joined the team in the dugout. The bench warmers hardly looked up, but manager Charlie Dressen came over and shook his hand.

"Glad to have you with us," he said briefly, and then turned his attention to the game, which was now in the second inning.

Willie sat down a little uneasily. He stole a glance down the bench and then gazed out at the Tigers in the field. There were some big names out there, players he had trained with who had a death grip on their positions: the great Al Kaline in right field, Rocky Colavito in left, Norm Cash at first, Dick McAuliffe at second, Billy Bruton in center. He felt happy and awed at the same time—happy that he was with such elite company, and awed at the audacity of his being there.

Surprisingly, Willie didn't have to wait long for action. In fact, he got into the game with unexpected suddenness. It was the fourth inning, the game was tied 5–5, and the Tigers were at bat. Hank Aguirre had been pitching for the Tigers and Dressen now lifted him for a pinch hitter. The little pepperpot manager turned to Horton.

"Hit for Aguirre," he said easily.

Willie Horton almost jumped out of his skin. He went to the bat rack, selected a war club and strode to the plate. He felt his heart pounding with excitement. He had not really expected to get into the game, but here he was, walking up to the plate for his first major league time at bat!

Ron Kline, a journeyman pitcher who had been around awhile, was on the mound for the Washington Senators. Horton stepped carefully into the batter's box, anchored himself there firmly and swung the bat in quick, sharp arcs. The thought passed through his mind that this was the big leagues, the big time, and this was tough major league pitching he was facing.

Kline went into his stretch, rocked a little and shot a fast ball over the outside corner. Willie watched it go by.

"Stuh-rike!" said the ump.

Willie backed out of the box, walked around nervously, then got back in. His hands were sweating and a frown creased his face. He had no idea what Ron Kline might throw him, but the situation was even because Kline didn't know what Willie might hit either.

Kline came in with another pitch, and this one seemed to Horton's liking. He swung and there was a loud crack as bat met ball. The ball traveled on a line into center field for a single—Willie Horton's first hit in the major leagues, delivered on his first turn at bat!

As it turned out, the hit had no importance to the game and the Tigers lost 9–8, but to Willie it was his biggest thrill in baseball.

Horton didn't get into another game until September 14, when the Tigers returned home to play the Baltimore Orioles. Willie was riding the bench again when the game started, and he was hoping that he would at least get into the game as a pinch hitter. There was a reason—his father was sitting in the bleachers in center field watching the game. Horton had tried to give him a pass to a grandstand seat, but his father preferred watching from the bleachers instead. It was where he'd always sat and he felt at home there.

Robin Roberts was on the hill for the Orioles, and he was doing a masterful job of stilling the Tiger bats. When the Tigers came up in the last half of the eighth inning, Baltimore had a 2-0 lead and Roberts had allowed only one hit.

The bottom part of the Detroit batting order was up, with catcher Gus Triandos leading off. Triandos lifted a foul fly and there was one away.

Gates Brown was the second man up and he walked. That brought up pitcher Jim Bunning.

Dressen looked down the bench. His creased face was serious. "Willie, bat for Bunning."

Horton's heart leaped, just as it had on his first major league trip to the plate. He selected a bat and walked slowly to the plate. The PA system announced his name and there was polite applause, but not much of it because Detroit fans still didn't know much about Willie Horton or his capabilities. In the bleachers, Horton's father stiffened with interest.

Roberts, having stifled the Tigers all through the game, decided he could get ahead of this raw rookie with a fast strike on the first pitch. He couldn't have been more wrong. The pitch came in, Willie swung at it and the ball shot high and far into left field. It landed 400 feet away in the upper deck and Horton rambled around the bases, with Gates Brown ahead of him, to tie the score!

If the single he had delivered on his first time at bat in Washington was a thrill, this one was doubly so. He clattered back into the dugout and a lot of old hands in the game patted him on the back. Willie felt a warm, satisfying glow as he sat down on the bench again.

When Horton's smash landed in the seats, his father leaped to his feet in his excitement and yelled, "That's my boy down there! That's my boy, Willie!"

A group of men around him looked at him with doubt. One of them said, "If that's your boy down there, what are you doing up here?"

"I *like* the bleachers," the elder Horton shot back.

The Tigers went on to win the game, 3–2, and the atmosphere in the Oriole clubhouse was funereal. Robin Roberts sat frowning in front of his locker, remembering the tremendous blast that had ruined his shutout and his victory.

"Who is that big guy?" he asked, over and over.

The answer—Willie Horton—was in the Tiger clubhouse surrounded by inquisitive sportswriters who didn't know who he was either.

"That's your first major league homer, isn't it?" one asked.

"Yeah. That's the first one."

"Were you nervous up at the plate?"

Willie grinned broadly—a wide, handsome grin that was typical. "Naw!" he said, with mock bravado in his voice. "I wasn't scared at the plate. I didn't get nervous until I got back in the dugout."

In a corner of the clubhouse manager Charlie Dressen was holding court with a group of baseball writers. He was chuckling happily over Horton's contribution.

"He's my Baby Campanella," he said. "He looks just like Roy Campanella, and someday he'll hit like him too."

"Where do you expect to use him?" asked a writer.

Dressen hesitated. "I don't know. We're battling for fourth place and I have to play the veterans as long as we have a chance to make fourth. But Willie's a fine hitter and I'd like him in there. I'll have to find a place for him."

Dressen eventually found a place for him. In the remaining games of the season, Horton continued to do well. The day after his homer he batted for Frank Lary and failed to hit—the first time in three at-bats that he did not deliver. Two days later he batted for Hank Aguirre and drove in the tying run with a sharp single. With a 3-for-4 record as a pinch hitter, Dressen started Willie in left field in a game with the Minnesota Twins at Bloomington. He went 0-for-4, but this was no particular disgrace since the entire Tiger team collected only two hits.

When the season ended, with the Tigers in a tie for fifth place with the Cleveland Indians, Horton's statistics were highly acceptable. He had appeared in 15 games, had 14 hits out of 43 times at bat for an average of .326, and had driven in four runs. His home run off Robin Roberts was the only one he got, but he had two doubles and a triple.

Although Horton's brief record created a stir of excitement in the Tiger front office, general manager Jim Campbell was not exactly enchanted with the Tigers as a team. He had hoped for a higher finish than fifth place, and when the season ended, he laid his plans on the line to newspapermen.

"The team finished fast, and that's fine," he said. "But we still have a basic rebuilding job ahead of us."

Named as the most expendable players were such outstanding performers as Norm Cash, Jim Bunning, Hank Aguirre and Rocky Colavito. Campbell was in the mood to trade.

That fall Campbell spent many hours on the telephone, talking to other general managers in the league. Then, on November 18, 1963, the bomb fell. The Tigers traded outfielder Rocky Colavito and pitcher Bob Anderson to the Kansas City Athletics for second baseman Jerry Lumpe and pitcher Ed Rakow. The two important men in the deal were Colavito and Lumpe.

Peddling Colavito to another team said something about Willie Horton's chances. Apparently the Tigers felt they could dispense with Colavito's services because they fully expected Horton to make the team in 1964. At least, from Horton's point of view, that was the most pleasant way to look at it.

"There's no doubt about it," Horton told Patricia. "It makes it easier for me to make the team as the left fielder next spring. I'm sure going to give it a whale of a try."

Willie Horton prepared for the big try by playing winter ball again in the Florida Instructional League. As a member of the Dunedin team, he led the league in runs-batted-in, and on one occasion in Sarasota he hit the longest home run of his career by blasting a ball over the left field wall of the Sarasota ballpark 375 feet away, clearing it by at least 50 feet. The ball not only passed over the wall but sailed over a garage at least 75 feet beyond the fence!

"That *was* a pretty good one," he admitted modestly.

Willie went home after the winter season ended and idled himself about the house until it was time to report to spring training at Lakeland. The inactivity and eating too heartily were big mistakes. When he reported to training camp he stepped on the scales and the hand moved to 219 pounds!

Manager Charlie Dressen, who knew Horton's capabilities and didn't want him to dissipate them by overweight, blew his top.

"I want you down to 197 pounds and I want it fast," he said. "You're going to run that blubber off!" He looked with distaste at the bulging Horton. "Why do you eat so much anyway?" he demanded.

"I'm not a big eater," Horton said stoutly.

"Then how do you get so big?"

Horton hesitated. "I don't know. I guess maybe it was those snacks and things watching television."

"Well," said Dressen, "you'd better watch yourself. You can take it off now, but as you get older you won't take it off so easily."

Horton worked at reducing for two horrifying weeks. He ate modestly and he ran in the hot Florida sun until the sweat poured off his body and his uniform became a sickly gray color. He rolled in the dirt like a rubber doll, did situps, pushups, rocked on his stomach and went through other tortures. Shortly before the ordeal was over, Willie came in from a run with sweat pouring down his face. A reporter stopped him.

"How's it going Willie?"

Horton sighed. "Man, I'm never going to let myself get this way again," he said with feeling.

"What do you weigh now?"

"I guess I'm down to two hundred by now," Willie said.

"What does Charlie Dressen want you to weigh?"

"About 197."

"You're running a lot and watching your diet, eh?"

"I sure am. But it's hard, let me tell you. I don't exactly dream, but some nights I just lay there in bed thinking of chocolate cake and cold milk."

But Horton never complained. He knew Charlie Dressen was right, and already there was a fondness growing between the two men. Horton knew Dressen had faith in him and wanted him to do well, and Willie didn't want to let him down.

"I haven't known Charlie long," he told the reporter, "but in the short time I have he's been like a father to me. I'd do anything for him. I haven't cheated once on him while I've been trying to reduce either."

"Not once?"

"Well, you know how Mr. Dressen makes chili in the clubhouse every once in a while. He slipped me a bowl last week. But that's all I've had, besides slim meals."

"You never had any more?"

"Well," Willie hedged, "I sorta had a bottle of pop to go with it."

When the two-week period was up, however, Willie Horton had reached his goal. He was now a svelte 197 pounds, having shed 22 pounds in 14 days. Dressen grinned when he saw the arrow on the scale tremble at 197. At once he cornered Hal Middlesworth, public relations director for the Tiger club.

"Tell you what," he said. "Go out and buy me a 22-pound ham. I want to present it to Horton."

Middlesworth got the ham and the next day Dressen gave it to Horton.

"That's how much you took off," he said. "I'll tell you how to cook it. But just one thing—don't eat the whole ham at one time!"

Chapter 5

Although the rigorous two-week training program reduced Willie Horton's waistline, it didn't seem to diminish his strength. When the spring training games began, Horton started to hit the ball with authority. He was making his bid for a permanent job in left field, and the bid was a strong one. In a doubleheader with the Chicago White Sox, he powered two home runs—one in the ninth inning of the opener with one on that gave Detroit a 2–1 victory, the other a solo homer that gave pitcher Mickey Lolich a one-run lead and started the Tigers to a 3–0 victory. On another occasion he hit a home run to defeat the Philadelphia Phillies.

"I'm surprised," he said after he hit it. "I felt kinda weak out there."

That caused a big laugh. One Tiger player said, "Willie's a hypochondriac. He always thinks he's sick or hurts somewhere. But he plays better with all his illnesses than we do in good health."

Horton, who had finished the previous season with the Tigers hitting well and was continuing it in spring training, nevertheless respected major league pitching.

"There's no doubt about it, major league pitching is a lot tougher," he said to a writer. "They try to make you hit their pitch, out on the corners or in tight. If you get overanxious, they've got you. That's my main trouble now—I get overanxious."

One day the Tigers had an exhibition game scheduled with the Los Angeles Dodgers, and in this game Willie had his first look at the talented offerings of Don Drysdale. The first time up Willie swung three times and struck out, the last pitch cutting the outside corner. On the second time up he fanned again—on the same outside pitch.

Willie went back to the dugout and began to think. *I'm trying to pull the ball,* he decided, *and he's nailing me on the outside pitch. What I should do is go with the pitch and hit it to right.*

The third time up he faced Drysdale and put his plan into operation—and lashed a double into right field.

In the dugout Dressen said, "That's the mark of a good hitter—to figure things out for himself."

The next day Horton arrived an hour early for practice and asked coach Bob Swift, who had managed Horton in Syracuse but who had been moved up as a coach for the Tigers under Dressen, to throw some outside pitches to him. In his next game he hit an outside pitch by John Buzhardt of the Chicago White Sox over the right field wall!

"He's learning," gloated Dressen. "That was a Babe Ruth type home run."

Willie Horton was rapidly dispelling any doubts about his ability to hit long and often, but since hitting is only one phase of baseball, the Tiger coaches began concentrating on making a good defensive outfielder out of him, too. Pat Mullin, who had been an outfielder for the Tigers and was now coaching, gave a lot of good advice to Willie. And Willie was not only appreciative but surprised at what he didn't know about fielding.

"I want to offer a few tips on fielding," Mullin told him one day. "If a fly is hit to you with runners on base, they'll take advantage of any waste motion to run on you. For example, I've seen you catch a fly, then take a couple of steps before you release the ball. That wastes precious time. You've got to get the ball away faster."

"I guess I didn't realize I was taking those extra steps," said Horton in surprise.

"Well, you were. When a fly ball is hit to you with men on base, back off a step or two, then move in at the last moment to make the catch. That puts you in a position to peg the ball, because you're coming in on it."

Horton nodded. Fundamentals. Fundamentals he had known and forgotten; others he had never known. And every one made sense.

"Another thing," said Mullin. "If you're going to have to make a throw after you catch a fly, field the ball off your right shoulder. You save precious seconds getting the ball away if you're ready to throw. If you catch the ball high or on your left side, you have to bring it across your body before you let it go—and that wastes time. It could mean the difference between a man scoring from third or being thrown out at the plate."

Horton took the advice seriously and tried to improve himself. "You know," he said, "Pat Mullin was always one of my idols. That's why I'm glad to be with Detroit. The men I admired are now teaching me. Why, when I first reported, Mullin handed me some reading material, and he's been helping me ever since. He's taught me how to play my position and told me things I've heard of but forgotten—and some things I *never* heard of."

As spring training progressed and Horton continued to get

long hits, his enormous strength began to take on a legendary character.

"He just might be the strongest man in baseball," Dressen said reflectively.

A couple of spring training incidents seemed to prove the point. One day there was a scuffle between the Tigers and an opposing team, and one of the enemy players had pitcher Joe Sparma's neck under his arm. Coach Frank Skaff, a big man, tried to break the grip and couldn't do it. Horton moved in and broke it, almost tearing off the opposing player's arm in the process. On another occasion Willie lost his temper when someone in the stands hurled an insult at him. Horton started for the seats—something a ballplayer is never supposed to do—and Tiger pitcher Denny McLain tried to stop him by leaping on his broad back. Horton carried McLain thirty feet without even breaking his stride. At that point another teammate, Mickey Stanley, tried to grab Horton's arm. Willie flicked his arm as if an insect was bothering him, and Stanley sprawled on the ground fifteen feet away.

By this time, the spectator who had thrown the insult had beaten a hasty retreat.

Despite a major contribution by young Willie Horton, the Tigers had only a so-so record during the spring training games. They started out by losing most of the early games, then picked up a little speed later on, but they ended their Grapefruit League competition with 10 wins and 17 losses. During those games Willie hammered out 6 home runs and batted in 18 in an impressive display of power and consistency that had Dressen's wrinkled face wreathed in smiles most of the time.

"He's a comer," Dressen said. "Right now I wouldn't trade Horton for Tony Oliva of the Twins." It was quite a statement at the time, because Oliva was considered the hottest new player in baseball and was destined, although no one knew it then, to win the batting championship in 1964 and 1965.

When the Tigers broke camp and headed north, Willie Horton was with them. He was delighted about staying with the team and really had only one minor complaint with his lot—he had lost his lucky chestnut.

"I don't think you need it," Al Kaline told him.

"But I like to have something lucky with me," said Horton.

On the way north the team stopped to play an exhibition game with the Knoxville Smokies. Before the game the same groundskeeper who had given Horton the first chestnut handed him another.

"That's to keep the good luck flowing," he said.

Willie chuckled and put it in his pocket. That day he hit a key double that drove in the winning run for the Tigers.

"I guess I'm superstitious about that chestnut," he said in the clubhouse, laughing at himself but still feeling rather serious about it.

By the time the Tigers reached Detroit to open the season against the Kansas City Athletics, practically everyone connected with baseball knew about the twenty-one-year-old slugger named Willie Horton. General manager Jim Campbell was particularly high on him.

"Willie looks like the best young hitter we've had since Al Kaline," he said.

Dressen agreed. "He's a good hitter now, and he's going to get better. You can bet he'll become one of the great right-hand hitters in the game."

Horton took these accolades humbly. Just before the season started he spoke to a reporter as he sat on a stool in front of his locker.

"I thank God for giving me the strength and ability to hit a ball a long way," he said somberly. "I thank Him for giving me my health so I can take advantage of this big chance. Playing baseball is all I know how to do, and it's all I ever want to do. I never really thought I'd get this chance so quick. I mean, I figured I'd have to spend lots of years in the minor leagues. Sometimes I lay in bed at night and think about it, and it seems like a dream. I just can't believe, sometimes, that it's happening to me."

Willie Horton waited eagerly for opening day at Tiger Stadium. With his fine spring training record, he felt certain he had won a permanent job in left field. But what he did not know was that Dressen was planning to platoon him with Billy Bruton, going with Bruton against right-handers and Horton against left-handers. Horton heard of the plan just before the regular season opened.

"Shucks," he said in disappointment. "I'm strongest against right-handed pitching, not left. I maybe don't hit quite as well against right-handers because I haven't faced many yet. But give me time, man, give me time."

Dressen fully intended to give Willie time, but not immediately. When opening day came around, it was Billy Bruton who started in left field and Horton remained on the bench.

It was a crushing blow to Willie's pride. His father and mother and several other relatives had shown up for the opener to see Willie play, and Willie felt badly about disappointing them. He wanted to please his parents by winning a job with the club, and he felt frustrated and embarrassed when his name was not in the starting lineup.

But he didn't play that day and when a sportswriter asked him how he felt about it, he spoke honestly.

"Sure, I'm disappointed," he admitted. "I thought I'd be in there. But heck—I'm just happy to be here with the team."

A few games later, when he was installed as a starter in a game, he felt strangely nervous and overanxious. He went hitless that day, and then he began to do what so many young players had done in the past—he started to press. The harder he tried the tighter he became, and finally he lost his timing, and his hitting was only a whisper of what it should have been.

All of a sudden the bottom had fallen out of Willie's promising world, and he was almost dazed by the experience. One time, when an opposing pitcher walked him, Willie stood at the plate as if in a trance. The umpire looked at him.

"That's ball four," the ump reminded him.

Willie was jarred back to reality and ran down to first. In the stands Jim Campbell shook his head. Dressen gritted his teeth in anguish at seeing his "Baby Campanella" reduced to such impotency.

Finally, after Willie had appeared in 25 games and batted only .163, Tiger management made a regretful decision.

"We're going to have to send you back to Syracuse," Dressen told him. "We think you'll get straightened out there. It may be tough to take now, but it will do you good. I haven't any doubt that you'll be back here."

Going back to the minors was a heavy blow to Willie's sagging morale. He had had a good spring training, and the newspapers had built him up as a coming star. Now all that was left were clippings—not very good clippings at that—and he was being sent back to the minors.

It took a while for the first sting of disappointment to wear off, but Willie was not one to cry quits and give up. When he went to Syracuse, it was with a renewed determination. He would play the kind of ball that would lift him right back into the majors where he belonged!

"I thought I'd stick this year," he admitted to his wife, "but now that I have to go back to the minors I'm going to have such a good year at Syracuse that they will never have to send me back again!"

Frank Carswell, who had managed Horton in Knoxville, was now piloting the Syracuse Chiefs, and he greeted the robust slugger with open arms.

"We're a little vulnerable to left-handed pitching," he said, "but with a right-hand hitter like you in the lineup, they won't be feeding us a diet of left-handers anymore."

"I'll do the best I can for you," Horton promised.

His "best" turned out to be very good indeed. Within a few days after he joined the Syracuse Chiefs, Wally Post, a veteran major league outfielder and long ball hitter who was finishing out his career with the Chiefs, spotted a flaw in Horton's batting stance.

"I think if you stand a little closer to the plate, you'll do better," he advised.

Horton took the advice, and immediately the hits began to drop in. In one three-game series against Rochester in late May he hit a single, a double, two triples and two home runs. Only one thing eluded him.

"I've never had a perfect day at bat in organized ball," he told his wife. "But every day you figure that this might be the time."

"It's bound to come," said Patricia, by now an avid and knowledgeable baseball fan.

After watching him for a month, manager Frank Carswell analyzed Willie's capabilities as a hitter for a reporter. "He doesn't try to pull the ball to left all the time—that's what's going to make him a great hitter. He hits the ball where it is pitched, and with many pitchers keeping the ball outside on him, Willie gets a lot of hits to right field. But he keeps the outfielders honest because he can hit to any field and hit with authority."

Willie Horton's world, which had collapsed so disastrously in Detroit, expanded to its normal shape in Syracuse. Everything now began to run in Willie's favor, including the fact that on June 2, 1964, Patricia Horton gave birth to a baby girl.

"We're naming her Terri Lynn," Willie said proudly. "We've got a boy and a girl now. I'm a happy man."

He stayed happy by having a fine season with Syracuse. As a key man in the Chiefs' offense, Horton hit .288 in 135 games, and smashed 28 home runs and batted in 99—even though he had missed a full month of the Syracuse season.

His performance suggested strongly that he would be the regular left fielder for the Tigers in 1965, but Willie was taking no chances. That winter he continued to play ball in Puerto Rico, as a member of the Mayaguez team under the direction of his former Syracuse manager, Bob Swift.

His hitting took up where it had left off at Syracuse, and by January 1, 1965, Horton was batting .312 and leading the league in home runs, runs-batted-in and doubles.

Then came tragedy.

Chapter 6

It was 9:00 A.M. on New Year's Day, 1965, and seven passengers were in a car traveling along the expressway between Detroit and Chicago. Among them were Clinton and Lillian Horton, Willie's parents. Visibility was impaired by a blinding snowstorm that swirled angrily around the car.

Suddenly, up ahead—and frighteningly close—a salt spreader blocked the road. There was a screech of brakes, but it was too late. The car smashed into the rear of the salt spreader, there was a sickening crunch of metal and then a dead silence. . . .

Mr. Horton was killed in the crash. Mrs. Horton was in serious condition in Sheldon Memorial Hospital in Albion, Michigan.

Willie Horton, his wife and two children had spent New Year's Eve at the home of Phillies outfielder Alex Johnson in Caguas, Puerto Rico. They were still there when the telegram came.

Willie felt the shock waves hit him hard and for a few minutes his mind failed to grasp the significance of the message he had received. His father killed, his mother near death! How could such a thing happen? They had had such a struggle in life, and just a few years ago he had purchased a new house for them. Things were a little easier now, and his parents were happy at the progress their son was making in baseball. His father, particularly, was always encouraging him to "keep hitting that ball."

And now this.

Swift arrangements were made to get Horton a flight from San Juan to Detroit. Because of the holiday traffic, they could get only one seat. Willie took it, and his wife and two children flew home the next day. Willie was met at Willow Run Airport near Detroit by Gates Brown, an outfielder from the Detroit Tigers and a long-time friend of Willie's.

"I'm so awfully sorry," Gates said lamely. "I don't know what more to say."

Horton nodded. He hardly heard the condolences. He was shaken badly, confused and grief-stricken and almost in a trance.

"My dad kept telling me that 1965 would be my year with the Tigers," he said. "Now he won't be here to see it."

Willie's mother died thirty-six hours after the crash. The double funeral was held a few days later.

Willie Horton had not yet recovered from his grief when it was time to report to the Tiger spring training camp in Lakeland, Florida. He went to camp with a heavy heart, but he also went with a new determination.

"I'm going to dedicate the 1965 season to my parents," he said to scout D'Annunzio. "If they play me in Florida, I'll make the team. I know I will."

"I think you will, too," said D'Annunzio.

But Horton hardly heard him. He was staring into space, still talking.

"I've got to do good just for the memory of my dad," he said. "He wanted so much for me to make good with the Tigers. And last year I flopped. This year, I've just got to make good. Whatever I do this year, I'm doing for my dad and mother."

Horton translated his confident words into action almost the moment he stepped onto the field in Lakeland. In batting practice and intrasquad games he hit the ball with power and he hit it often. Manager Charlie Dressen was delighted at what he saw. His Baby Campanella was showing every sign of being a player who, this year, would come into his own.

But even though he enjoyed a fine spring training, Willie grieved for his parents. When he talked about his mother and father he would choke up. One day he was talking to a sportswriter whom he knew well, and he stared out into left field wistfully.

"If I make the grade as the regular left fielder for the Tigers," he said, "there'll really be two men standing out there. One will be me and the other will be my dad. He kept telling me this would be my year, but he won't be around to see it. Even so, he'll be with me, out in left field and at the plate, at least in spirit."

To a ballplayer anxious to make good, baseball is an all-consuming passion that occupies his mind and heart, and it was a good thing for Willie that he had baseball to take his mind off his troubles. But just when baseball was beginning to crowd somber thoughts out of his mind, another tragedy occurred.

It was Sunday, March 7, and the Tiger A and B teams played an intrasquad game. After the game, Charlie Dressen spent four hours mixing the spring season's first batch of chili—a personal recipe that Dressen enjoyed cooking for his team. Willie was a little overweight again, but he ate a small portion of it. After the chili party was over, Dressen retired to his hotel room. The clock said 11:00 P.M.

At seven o'clock in the morning the phone rang in coach

Stubby Overmire's room. It was Dressen. "My wife is ill in Los Angeles," he said. "I'd like you to drive me to the airport."

Overmire got dressed, picked up Dressen, and drove him to the Tampa Airport. When they arrived Dressen went to a phone and called general manager Jim Campbell back at Lakeland. He told Campbell of the illness of his wife.

"I'll be back in a few days," he said. "Bob Swift can handle the team while I'm gone."

It was not until noon the next day that Campbell heard the truth. Dressen had actually suffered a heart attack in his room and, upon arrival in Los Angeles, had been taken immediately to Santa Monica Hospital.

The Tigers were on the field working out when Campbell called an emergency meeting in the clubhouse. He told the team of Dressen's serious illness. They were hopeful the manager could return to the club by opening day, but they were not certain. In the meantime, Bob Swift would be acting manager.

The news stunned the Tiger players, but Horton more than anyone else. To Willie, this was the second tragedy in a little over two months. Horton held a fierce loyalty to the peppery Dressen, who had already helped him over some rough spots.

"I sure hope he gets better," he said solemnly. "I really love that man. He's been like a father to me, especially since my real father is gone."

Shaken, the team went back onto the field. Two years before, when Dressen took over as manager, some of the players had resented him. But by now they realized what a firm baseball man he was, and appreciated the talents he brought to the game. First baseman Norm Cash put it as well as anybody.

"I think this team was just beginning to understand that man," he said.

Bob Swift took over the reins amidst a pall of gloom. As

usual, the sportswriters moved in on him to get his reaction. Swift just shook his head sadly.

"Managing a major league club is something I've always wanted," he admitted, "but I didn't want to get it this way. We'll have the midnight curfew and other rules that Dressen set up. Everything will be the same. My ideas are parallel to Charlie's."

As the team went to work again, the players began to realize how much they missed Dressen. But there was one bright spot in the situation. All the Tigers liked Bob Swift. Swift was a sound baseball man, having learned his trade as a catcher for the Tigers in the thirties and forties. He was tough, a guy you didn't fool around with, but he was respected and his relationship with the players was a warm and friendly one.

The day after Swift took over, the Tigers were scheduled to play their first Grapefruit League game with the Minnesota Twins. Swift mulled over the lineup, finally writing Willie Horton's name in as the left fielder.

"Once Willie gets his confidence—and he's getting it more every day—there won't be a ball park in America that can hold him," he said. "He'll hit 'em out in every direction—left, center and right. Maybe as many as forty of them a year."

It was true. Willie's confidence in his ability to do the job was improving every day. He now had a double reason for having a good season. First, he had dedicated the 1965 season to his dead parents, and he wanted to have the very best year he could. Second, he wanted to reward Dressen for the faith the manager had shown in him.

"I want to prove to Mr. Dressen that his faith in me was right," he said simply. "And along with it, I want to prove to myself and the Tiger fans that I'm worthy of wearing this Tiger uniform."

Horton started to prove himself in the first game of the exhibition season, and he continued throughout the Grapefruit season. On one occasion the Tigers met the Chicago White Sox, and a trio of Chicago pitchers shut the Tigers out for eight innings. As the Tiger ninth came up, Chicago clung to a perilous one-run lead.

Up on the roof of the stadium stands were Larry Osterman, broadcaster for a Kalamazoo (Michigan) TV station, and general manager Jim Campbell. The idea was to have the camera at an angle that would catch the two men talking about Willie Horton and also take in Horton as he batted at home plate. The camera angle was just right as Horton stepped up to the plate in the ninth inning with a possible tying run on base.

As Horton settled himself in the batter's box, Osterman looked at Campbell.

"Jim," he said, "what do you think of this boy, Willie Horton?"

Before Campbell could frame an answer, Horton swung at the first pitch and slammed it over the right field fence—the wrong field for a right-handed hitter—to win the game for the Tigers, 2–1.

Campbell grinned. "What more can I say, Larry?"

End of broadcast.

Willie Horton hit around .300 during the exhibition season and when the team moved north he was a full-fledged member of it. Only one thing disturbed him. Acting manager Bob Swift was planning to platoon Horton with Jim Northrup, another promising young outfielder, using Horton against left-handers and Northrup against right-handers.

It was the same way he had started the 1964 season, and Willie worried about it. And as luck would have it, a right-hander was working for the Athletics when the Tigers opened their season against them in Kansas City. So Northrup was scheduled to play as Willie sat on the bench.

In the clubhouse before the Tigers took the field for the opener, Bob Swift read a telegram from Charlie Dressen.

"Loads of luck to all of you," it said. "I want you to know I appreciate the way you have performed for Bob Swift and the coaches during my illness. I hope all the hitters hit .300 and all the pitchers win 20 games. I will be following your play pretty closely now, but don't worry about me if you are thrown out at the plate on a close play. Take chances when the opportunity presents itself."

"He's a great little guy," Horton said to anyone who would listen. "I'm going to play hard for him—if and when I get in the lineup."

The Tigers offered a rather impressive lineup to open the 1965 season, and some of the experts were saying they would finish anywhere from second to fourth. Few would predict a pennant for the club, but they had the makings of a solid contender. Their infield consisted of Norm Cash at first base, Jerry Lumpe at second, Dick McAuliffe at shortstop, and Don Wert at third. The outfield saw Al Kaline in right, Don Demeter in center and Jim Northrup in left. The catcher was John Sullivan and the pitcher for the opener was Mickey Lolich.

The Tigers got away to a good start. They won their opening game, 6–2, and on the following day whipped Kansas City again, 11–4, to lead the league with a 2–0 record. Horton did not play in either game.

As the Tigers moved on to Minnesota to meet the Twins, Bob Swift said, "Our whole team is hustling. You win when you hustle."

The Tigers hustled another win in Minnesota, 6–4, for their third straight victory. A couple of rainouts occurred, then, and the Tigers found themselves in Los Angeles to meet the Angels. The Angels promptly put a crimp in their winning streak by defeating them 3–1.

It was not until the fifth game of the season that Willie Horton was inserted in the starting lineup. This was in the second game of the Los Angeles series. Horton was determined to do something to help the Tiger cause, as well as his own.

The game turned out to be a pitchers' battle, and at the end of nine innings the score was tied, 1–1. The two teams struggled through the tenth, eleventh and twelfth with no change in the score. By the time the thirteenth inning opened, it looked as if neither side would ever score another run.

Willie Horton was the first man up in the top of the thirteenth. He stepped carefully into the batter's box, swung his bat menacingly a couple of times, then cocked it over his right shoulder. Bob Lee, on the mound for the Angels, came in with the first pitch and Willie didn't wait. He drilled it into left field for a clean single.

It was only the second hit the Detroit team had managed in the game.

But now things started to jell. Jackie Moore, a rookie catcher, slapped a single to center field and Horton raced around second and into third.

That was the end of Lee's tenure on the mound, and in came George Brunet. If anybody was figured to quell a Tiger rally, it was Brunet. Although he had trouble with other clubs, he had a reputation for being poison to the Tigers.

But this time he fared badly. He uncorked a wild pitch and Horton raced home with the lead run. Before the inning ended the Tigers scored two more runs to go ahead 4–1—and that's the way the game ended.

Horton had managed only one hit in five times up, but it had started the Tigers' winning rally.

On April 21 the Tigers opened their home season with a 1–0 win over Kansas City. Horton played but failed to hit. The next day Swift had Northrup back in left field with Willie again riding the bench.

But on April 24 Horton started in left field and this time he made the most of his opportunity. The game against the Minnesota Twins was a close one, and when the Tigers went into the seventh the score was Twins 2, Tigers 1. Willie Horton came up in the inning with no one on base and lashed a long home run into the left field stands to knot the score at 2–2.

The Tigers added another run to make the score 3–2, but they saw the lead evaporate when the Twins scored two in the top of the ninth, putting them in front, 4–3. That placed the Tigers on the brink of defeat, with only the last of the ninth to do anything about it.

Horton did something. He laced his second home run of the game into the left field stands to tie it all up again, 4–4.

Then the Twins fell apart. They walked two men and pinch-hitter Gates Brown came up. He won the game, 7–4, with another round-tripper.

After that game, Bob Swift was faced with a real dilemma. Who was to play left field—Northrup, Horton or Brown? Northrup was a fine rookie with plenty of promise and deserved a chance. Horton was a menacing batter with the determination to pin down the left field job for himself. Brown, a weak fielder but a frightening long ball hitter, was making his bid.

"It's quite a problem," Swift admitted, but opposing managers weren't very sympathetic. "I wish I had a problem with those three guys," one moaned.

The next day Swift was puzzling over the lineup when a reporter said to Horton, "It looks to me as though you're trying to win the left field job by going for home runs."

Horton shook his head. There was as much awe in the motion as there was denial.

"Honest, I wasn't trying for homers. I was just trying to get base hits. I knew I hit both of them good, but I didn't know they were going out." It was as if he was surprised at his own power.

But the two home runs didn't get Horton anywhere—at least, not immediately. Swift went with Northrup in the next game, and with Brown in several others. And Horton sat on the bench wondering if he was really going to be able to deliver on his promises to his dead parents and the ill Charlie Dressen.

Chapter 7

By the end of April the Tigers were in second place with 8 wins and 4 losses, trailing the first place Minnesota Twins, who had an 8–3 record. On May 2 Willie Horton got back into the lineup, playing in the second game of a doubleheader against Boston. The Tigers dropped both games, but it wasn't Willie's fault that they lost the second one. He hit a single, double and triple in four times up—and the triple was a booming drive to deep center field. In the clubhouse after the game, Willie made a typical remark disparaging his accomplishment.

"I really didn't hit that triple very hard," he said. "I hit it down on the handle."

When Bob Swift heard the comment he grinned widely. "On the handle, eh? And he still hit it 430 feet! That boy just doesn't know how strong he is!"

"Well, how strong is he?" asked a sportswriter, fishing for a quote.

He got one. "I'm not going to try to find out how strong he is," Swift said. "I want him on my side."

But Horton wasn't running in luck, despite his fine day against

Boston. Right after the big game, Dr. Russell Wright, the Detroit team physician, operated on Willie's nose. He had been having trouble breathing and the doctor had found a growth in his nose that had to be removed. That put Horton back on the bench for three more days.

Bob Swift returned Willie to the lineup on May 8 when the Tigers met the Orioles in Baltimore. It was a long, drawn-out 15-inning game, won by the Tigers on a homer by Al Kaline. Horton was helpless at the plate. He went 0-for-7.

"Man! My timing's off or something!" he complained.

The next day Baltimore whipped the Tigers twice, 7–1 and 5–4, dumping them into sixth place. In the first game Horton went 0-for-4, but in the second he hit a home run and a single in five tries. The following day Horton went 0-for-4 again as the Tigers lost, 5–4. Horton, despite all the promise and potential that everyone knew he had, was not being impressive with the bat. In the last 20 times at bat he had managed only two hits, and there were cynics in Detroit who began to wonder if Horton would again be sent back to Syracuse.

Then came May 11.

Before the game between Detroit and the Senators at Washington, Mike Roarke, one of the Tiger coaches trying to help Willie get untracked, got him aside at the batting cage.

"Keep your top hand over," he said, swinging a bat to show Horton what he meant. "You've been letting your right hand drag when you swing, and you're not getting all of your power into your swing."

Horton tried the advice during batting practice and hit several long drives. Just before the Tigers took the field, with Horton slated to start in left field, Roarke slapped Willie on the seat of his pants.

"Big man," he said, "let's get a couple tonight."

The Tigers started out badly and so did Horton. In the first six innings Detroit failed to score, and when the seventh came around they were trailing Washington 6–0. Willie had been helpless in three trips to the plate. He had reached first safely in the second inning on an infield error. In the fourth he grounded weakly to third base. In the sixth he stood with the bat on his shoulder and was called out on strikes.

In the top of the seventh inning the Tigers mounted a rally. They loaded the bases with eager runners, and Don Demeter unloaded them with a double to left center. Later Demeter scored from third on a ground ball by Kaline.

That made the score Washington 6, Detroit 4.

With four runs in and the bases empty, it was Willie Horton's turn to bat. Jim Duckworth was on the mound for the Senators and he worked cagily on the big slugger. It was a ball, a strike, a ball and then one over the outside corner. Horton swung and the crack of the bat was like the report of a rifle. The ball rose in a high arc and came down on the other side of the left field fence, 420 feet away. The hit made the score Washington 6, Detroit 5.

The score remained that way until the Tigers came to bat in the ninth. Third baseman Don Wert opened the inning with a walk. Ron Kline, now working for the Senators, struck out Jim Northrup. But Don Demeter came through with a single, and there were runners on first and second. Kaline grounded out and the runners moved to second and third.

The tying and potential winning runs were now in position to score on a solid hit.

Gil Hodges, the Washington manager, trudged slowly from the dugout. On the mound he put a quick question to Ron Kline.

"Horton's up next," he said. "Do you want to pitch to him or put him on?"

"I'll pitch to him," said Kline.

Hodges nodded and returned to the dugout. Willie Horton

stepped up to bat, took a couple of practice swings, and cocked the bat over his right shoulder. Kline went into his stretch and delivered the ball.

"Stuh-rike!" grunted the umpire.

Willie stepped out, got back in. Kline stretched again. A fast ball screamed in.

"Stuh-rike tuh!" said the ump.

Horton frowned. He rubbed dirt on his hands. Again he returned to the batter's box. Kline went up with his arms, came in with the pitch. Horton swung.

It was not a home run, but it was a line single to left field that scored two runs and put the Tigers ahead 7–6. And that's the way the game ended.

In the clubhouse Willie had a handsome smile pasted across his face. The single was the really clutch hit of the two, but the long home run also pleased him.

"Maybe I'm back in the groove again," he commented.

"Duckworth must be talking to himself in the other clubhouse," said a reporter jokingly.

Willie's head came up sharply. "Who's Duckworth?" he asked.

He was not being funny. Horton had difficulty recalling names or dates, and he simply didn't know the name of the pitcher off whom he had clouted his long home run.

That night, after the game, some of the Tiger players and a couple of sportswriters had a late snack at Rosco's, a popular restaurant in Washington. The conversation turned to Willie's performance in the game.

"He'll hit forty home runs some year, as soon as he gets wise to the pitching up here," said Jerry Lumpe. "When Willie hits a ball he gets top spin on it, the way Mickey Mantle does, and the ball carries."

"He could be another Harmon Killebrew," said Don Wert. "He'll hit 'em as far as anyone in the league before he's through."

Gates Brown, Horton's roommate and a good friend, sat there shaking his head.

"Me, when I hit a homer, I pull the ball," he said with awe. "But not Willie. He just hits 'em and they go out in any direction—left, center or right. If I had his power I'd hit fifty home runs a year and make myself seventy grand." He shook his head again. "And you know something about Willie? He worries that he won't make the lineup. Every night he worries whether Swift will put him in the game the next day. He's a real worrier."

One of the sportswriters then popped an interesting question.

"Do you think Willie is the strongest man in baseball?"

The players pondered the question a moment.

"I think he might be," said one player. "Of course, that guy Howard is pretty strong too." He was referring to Washington's Frank Howard.

"I wonder what would happen," a reporter mused, "if Willie Horton and Frank Howard met some night in a dark alley."

Don Demeter took a nip at his sandwich. "The alley would lose," he said.

During batting practice the next day, Bob Swift sat in the Tiger dugout and penciled Willie's name in the lineup.

"I've come to the conclusion that Horton can hit right-handers as well—and maybe better—than left-handers," he said. "So Willie is my left fielder from now on, no matter who pitches. He's out there to stay, and I hope he stays until 1985."

"I'm glad to hear that," Horton said when he heard Swift's appraisal, "because I'm really developing a bad hitting habit out there that I'll have to control. I don't know how it happens but lately, when I swing at the ball, I lose control of the bat and I swing one-handed."

"Did you hit that home run yesterday with one hand?" asked a reporter slyly.

"Yeah. I guess I did."

The reporter went away smiling. Willie was always downgrading himself. How many guys in the league could hit a 420-foot homer with one hand? "I suppose," said the reporter to a friend, "he lost control of the bat in the ninth inning when he drove in the tying and winning runs with a single, too!"

In the second game of the series the Washington Senators started Mike McCormick on the mound. In the second inning, Horton led off with a single. In the fourth he clouted a 400-foot home run over the left center field wall, and in the eighth drove in a run with his second single. The Tigers won, 5–2, with Willie leading the way.

In typical fashion, Willie Horton had a built-in excuse despite his good night at the bat.

"Since my nose operation, I've been feeling a little woozy," he said. "But I've been drinking a lot of fruit juice and I'll be strong again soon."

Gates Brown chuckled at the comment. "I wish I was weak like Willie," he said.

The next night Willie Horton continued his ferocious bombardment of Washington pitching. In the first inning he was walked intentionally. In the second he hit a bases-empty home run off Pete Richert—a 390-footer to left center. In the fourth he hit his second home run—a 420-footer into right center—with two on base, off Jim Duckworth, whose name he wasn't quite sure of. And in the sixth he walloped a double to drive in another run.

He ended the evening's festivities with two homers, a double and five runs-batted-in as the Tigers romped to a 13–3 victory.

The two home runs made it four in three nights.

The Tigers packed their bags after sweeping the Washington series and headed for Boston. When they arrived in Beantown every writer in the city beat a path to Willie Horton's locker. Suddenly this young man from the ghettos of Detroit was an important public figure—for by this time it was obvious that Willie Horton was on a fantastic hitting spree such as had not been seen in years.

Willie was half-embarrassed at the attention everyone was paying him, and he tried to answer questions honestly and sincerely. But he always felt better when the interviews were over and he was back on the field with a bat in his hand. The field was his element.

The Boston Red Sox were hoping that Horton had left his game in Washington and had now run out of steam, but in the first game at Fenway Park their hopes were rudely shattered.

Boston jumped away to a two-run lead off the Tigers' Denny McLain in the first inning, after the Tigers had failed to score in the top half. Horton was leadoff man in the second inning and, in his usual robust manner, smashed a ball at Boston shortstop Eddie Bressoud that was so vicious it spun him around in his tracks. Horton beat it out for a hit while Bressoud was trying to figure out where first base was.

"He looked like he got caught in a revolving door," was a comment in the press box.

The hit was wasted, though, and the Tigers failed to score in the second. Boston then came to bat in the last half of the second and scored three more runs to make it Boston 5, Detroit 0. Then Willie really went to work.

In the top of the third Horton came to bat with Al Kaline on second. This time Willie pickled a pitch by Bob Heffner and drilled it into the left center bullpen. The hit was the big blow in a five-run rally that tied the game, 5–5.

In the fourth inning Horton was hit by a pitched ball and a wag in the stands said, "That's one way to stop him from hitting —put him on first."

Boston went ahead, 6–5, in the last of the fifth, but in the top of the sixth the Tigers rallied again. They got three runs to go ahead, 8–6, and what was the crowning blow? It was Willie Horton's second home run of the game—a long drive off Jack Lamabe into the center field bleachers with Kaline on!

That made the record six home runs in four nights!

But the game wasn't over. The Red Sox were having a field day with Tiger pitching, too, and they bounced back in the last of the seventh to tie up the game, 8–8.

In the eighth Horton was up again, and this time he stepped completely out of character. He struck out against Dick Radatz, but did it with three classic swings that stirred up the air so violently that, as one reporter put it, the "steeple on the Old North Church almost toppled."

The Tigers finally won the game, 12–8, in the tenth inning, and Horton had a hand in that, too. Willie contributed a single to the rally to drive in Kaline from second.

When the carnage was over, Horton's record looked like this: Willie had hit two home runs, two singles, scored three times, knocked in five runs for the second night in a row, grabbed the home run lead in the American League with nine, took over the batting lead with a .383 average and shoved his slugging average up to a phenomenal .900. And, probably more important from a team standpoint than anything else, he had gotten on base 15 of the last 17 times at bat.

In the clubhouse, Horton was again mobbed by newspapermen. Once more he tried to answer all questions politely and accurately, but the most poignant thing he said, the thing that sent all of them away with a touch of sadness, was this simple statement.

"I just hope," he said, "that the Man Upstairs lets my dad and mom see this."

When the clubhouse had quieted down, outfielder Lenny Green said, "Willie is just like Mantle and Killebrew. When he hits that ball it just keeps going and going and going."

Umpire Larry Napp, who had worked behind the plate, said, "Horton got his first two hits one-handed. One of them was that long home run. I wonder what will happen when he learns to keep both hands on the bat?"

Willie chuckled. "That's that bad habit I told you I was getting into," he said. "But I really think I'm a better hitter this year than last. Last year I was pressing too much. I'm growing out of that. I'm trying not to listen to the other hitters as much. Sometimes a guy would come back from the plate and say something about what the pitcher was throwing and what to look for. Then I'd get all fouled up, waiting for a certain pitch. Now I'm going up there with an open mind. Another thing I've learned—I move around in the batter's box more. Against a pitcher with a lot of good breaking stuff, I move up in the box to hit it before it breaks. What it comes down to, really, is that God is helping me. He has answered my prayers and is giving me the good season I wanted for my dad and mom."

Before the Tigers returned to their hotel for the night, Don Demeter gathered a few of the boys around him.

"Listen, fellows," he said. "We can't let anything happen to Willie, right? So who's volunteering to guard him tonight? I'll take the first watch."

Willie just grinned—the wide, handsome grin that he could always manufacture when he was feeling good.

Chapter 8

Although the Tigers were on the road, all of Detroit was talking about Willie Horton. The TV broadcasters entered the excitement by calling him Willie the Wonder. And whenever the TV screen showed him circling the bases after hitting one out of the park, the words "Willie the Wonder" flashed on the screen.

In the Tiger dugout, closer to the scene of action, the Tiger players began to play a game. When Willie came to bat they would start a countdown. "Ten . . . nine . . . eight . . . seven . . ." The idea was to reach zero at blastoff time, just when Willie swung and knocked the ball out of the park. It was a game to see who came closest to the precise moment when Willie connected with the ball.

"You guys!" was all Willie could think of to say in his half-embarrassment.

The next day, May 15, the Tigers and Red Sox clashed again. The Red Sox threw an up-and-coming twenty-two-year-old pitcher named Jim Lonborg against the Tigers in an effort to cool off the rampaging Horton. The Tigers failed to score in the top of the first and Boston got Lonborg a one-run lead in the bottom half.

Willie Horton was the leadoff batter in the second inning. He stepped carefully into the batter's box, flexed his huge muscles and waited for Lonborg's delivery. Lonborg was cautious, getting a pitch outside, one inside and one on the corner. Then he delivered a fourth pitch to Horton and big Willie swung. The ball went on a line to deep left field.

Felix Mantilla, left fielder for the Sox, raced back for the drive, but the ball went over his head and crashed against the scoreboard. By the time the ball was retrieved, Willie was safely standing on second base. Singles by Don Demeter and Bill Freehan brought him home, and Demeter scored later on a passed ball. The Tigers had grabbed a 2–1 lead.

In the third inning Willie came up with a man on first base and Lonborg did the near-impossible—he got him to bounce into a double play. The roar that went up from the Boston fans at this achievement could be heard all over Massachusetts.

In the sixth Horton again led off, and this time he singled. He died on first when Tiger batters were unable to push him around. In the eighth he singled again, this time with Kaline on first, and in the ninth he hit a long sacrifice fly to score a runner from third.

The Tigers won the game, 6–2, and Willie had three hits out of four times to push his batting average to .406 and his slugging average to .906. He had collected 15 hits in his last 19 times at bat for an average of .789, and he didn't show any signs of cooling off.

Again there was a crowd of sportswriters around Horton's locker after the game, and Al Kaline, star of the Tigers for a dozen years, sat alone shaking his head.

"I never saw a player get this hot in my life," he said. "And it's not going to his head either."

"What if he keeps this up until the end of the year?" asked Gates Brown. "What'll he end up with?"

The question sent one newspaper man scurrying into the realm of mathematics. "If he keeps it up," he said finally, "he will have 28 doubles, 9 triples, 81 home runs, 187 runs-batted-in and certain enshrinement in Cooperstown."

It was obvious, of course, that no player could maintain such a blistering pace forever, and the only question in anyone's mind was when his streak would come to an end. Willie, himself, wasn't worried about it. He was more worried by the attention he was receiving from the press.

It was after the departure of the reporters that day that Willie sauntered over to Al Kaline's locker. "Al," he said, "can we talk a few minutes?"

"Sure. What about?"

"The writers," said Horton simply. "They make me awful nervous. I just don't know what to say to them."

Kaline smiled. His mind went back to his early days in the league, when he had won the batting championship at the tender age of twenty. He had been the target of newspaper and magazine writers and had been shy and ill at ease in their presence. Learning to handle them had come slowly, but it had come.

"I know how you feel, Willie," he said. "I was the same way for a long time. But I found out that all you have to do is be honest with them. Tell them the truth and don't criticize any of the other team's players."

Horton went back to his locker, thinking about what Kaline had said. He knew that he would have to learn to talk to the writers, that this was part of his job, but he also knew that it would be a hard thing to master—much harder than hitting a baseball out of the park.

The rest of the Tigers recognized Horton's dilemma and tried to help. Some kidded him to keep him loose. "You really should be in a higher league," said Jerry Lumpe, and that got a laugh. But pitcher Dave Wickersham may have helped him the most. A deeply religious man, Wickersham counseled him on the satisfaction of reading the Bible. "You've had a tough time lately, with your folks dying and now all this publicity. The Bible will help ease your mind."

Detroit and Boston had a doubleheader scheduled for the next day, a Sunday, and old Fenway Park was bulging at the seams with customers, many of them attracted to the park to watch the amazing Willie perform. Earl Wilson, veteran Boston pitcher, was on the mound in the first game, and big Earl—six-foot-three and 215 pounds—was determined to stop Willie Horton. He succeeded in the first inning when Willie flied harmlessly to center, but it was in the fourth, after Boston had taken a 3–0 lead, that the fireworks started.

Kaline was the first man up in the fourth with Horton waiting in the on-deck circle. Wilson's first pitch was a brush-back that sent Kaline reeling into the dirt. The second one put Kaline down again, but on this occasion the ball hit Al's bat and dribbled to shortstop. Kaline was out at first.

Horton stepped into the batter's box, eyeing Wilson suspiciously. In baseball, a hitter is considered to have arrived if the pitchers begin to brush him back. The way Willie had been going, it was inevitable that somebody would begin to do this—and the somebody was Earl Wilson.

Wilson reared back and sent a pitch inside and high. Horton hit the dirt to get out of the way. He got up slowly, his eyes riveted on Wilson, and then he stepped in front of the plate in a threatening gesture.

Wilson came in off the mound a few steps. "Come on out here!" he challenged. "Just come on out here!"

Willie kept his cool. "If I do," he said slowly, "you can be moved, like a mountain."

It didn't occur to Willie that a man would have a difficult time moving a mountain, but moving the mountainous Earl Wilson was something Willie felt he could accomplish. The confrontation between the two brought all of the players onto the field but the melee was stopped without any blows being tossed. One reason was that Bob Swift ran straight for Willie and held him back.

"Take it easy," he kept saying. "Just take it easy."

Willie subsided, the players returned to their dugouts and Horton then struck out.

So far, Wilson had done what no other pitcher had done for the last week—he had held Horton hitless.

"I'll get him the next time," mumbled Willie in the dugout.

The next time was the seventh inning. Horton stepped into the batter's box and waved his bat menacingly. Wilson glared at Horton from the pitcher's hill. Then he reared back and fired a fast ball. Horton lashed it into left field for a double.

Willie grounded out in the ninth, giving him a 1-for-4 game—not quite up to recent standards. But then, none of the Tigers hit Wilson well; they lost the game, 5–0.

The second game was closer, but the Tigers lost that one by a 4–3 score. Horton got two doubles out of four tries to keep his streak alive.

After the doubleheader loss, the Tigers came home to friendly Tiger Stadium. The rampaging Horton had completed a stretch of games that became known as the "Seven Games in May"—a fierce and fantastic exhibition of power hitting that had firmly cemented his hold on the left field job. Willie Horton, after a so-so start, was now, without question, a real, honest-to-goodness major leaguer.

On May 17, the day of the Tigers' return home, Charlie Dressen returned to Detroit. He stepped off a DC-8 at Willow Run Airport flashing a wide smile. He could hardly contain himself when he was greeted by the Tiger brass.

"That Willie Horton!" he exclaimed. "He must really be something! Everybody in Los Angeles is talking about him—the radio announcers, newspapers, fans."

Dressen told the Tiger management that he could not take over immediate control of the club. The doctors had told him to watch for a week or so before assuming command. But that did not seem to be the important thing in Dressen's mind. Willie Horton was the important thing.

"The great thing about Horton is that he'll get better," he said enthusiastically. "Once he learns the pitchers he'll be a great hitter. You can't put a forty-year-old head on a twenty-two-year-old boy, but Willie is learning fast."

Despite Horton's personal hitting streak, the Tigers were not doing well as a team. They were playing only .500 ball and were battling to stay in the first division. On May 18, with Dressen watching from the stands, the Tigers did their best to bring off a victory in celebration of Dressen's return to health. But it didn't work out. Washington won a wild slugfest, 15–9.

But Willie enjoyed another good game. He had a single and a triple in four times, lifting his batting average to a sizzling .408 and maintaining a slugging average of .895.

"My Baby Campanella," said Dressen, grinning.

During the early part of the season Detroit had exhibited a curious inability to win doubleheaders, having dropped four straight. In late May they met the Baltimore Orioles in a twin bill and again dropped both games. Horton had one hit and sat out the second game. Then he went hitless three days in a row.

At this point the Tigers needed a boost in morale and they

received it on May 30. That was the day Charlie Dressen returned as manager of the team. Everyone was glad to see him back.

"He's as spry as ever," remarked one player.

"He looks great," said another.

Willie Horton said nothing, but he was particularly glad to see Dressen back at the helm. He appreciated the peppery little manager as much as, or more than, anyone on the team. Dressen was a second father to Horton, and Willie appreciated how Dressen had helped him with his problems and encouraged him continually.

On the day Dressen returned, the Tigers played a doubleheader with New York, and split. They were in third place, behind Minnesota and Chicago. Then, as June got under way, the Tiger hitters suddenly slumped. They seemed unable to buy a run. In one horrendous stretch they went 23 innings, scoring only one run in all that time—and that was a solo homer by Horton. And by June 10 they were five games behind Minnesota with a significant series coming up between the two teams. It was a four-game set-to, and the Tigers had a chance to move up close to first place if they could sweep the series.

The Minnesota Twins disabused the Tigers of that idea right away by winning the first two games, both by 5–4 scores.

"We've got to do something about that," said Willie, voicing the obvious. "We win the next two and we're no worse off than when the series started. And the year is young yet."

Horton began to do something about that as soon as the third game of the series started. With the score tied at 2–2 in the bottom of the second, Don Wert singled, Jerry Lumpe singled and Horton rapped his twelfth homer of the season to give the Tigers a 5–2 lead. It was his thirty-sixth run-batted-in and tied him with Al Kaline for the club lead. The Tigers won the game, 8–5.

In the last game of the four-game series the Twins sent their star hurler, Jim Kaat, to the mound. The Tigers managed to edge the Twins, 5–4, but one of the interesting sidelights of the game occurred when Horton stepped up to bat in the fourth.

Earl Battey, the Minnesota catcher, squinted up at Horton. "Hey," he said. "How about letting me have your four tickets?"

Horton looked at him dubiously. "What four tickets?"

"Your four tickets to the All-Star Game."

Willie grunted. "I'm not getting four tickets to the All-Star Game," he said.

"Yes, you are. Every player on the team gets four tickets."

Horton grunted again. "I don't expect to be on the team," he said candidly.

Horton then swung on a Jim Kaat fast ball and rode it out of the park to help the Tigers post their victory.

Horton believed what he said. There had been speculation that he would be voted to the All-Star team, but Horton had paid little attention to it. In fact, there was speculation he might win the American League batting championship, too, since he was hanging close to .370 and showing no signs of a serious letup.

"The thing that makes Horton a good hitter," explained Dressen one day, "is the fact that he knows what the pitchers are trying to do to him. After that spree he went on in May, they've been feeding him breaking pitches and change-ups on the outside part of the plate. So Willie has responded by not swinging for the fences. He waits on nearly every pitch and keeps lashing line drive singles and doubles—often to right field."

Willie, however, paid little attention to all this talk. In the clubhouse a reporter asked him what he thought his chances of winning the batting title might be.

"I don't really know," he said honestly.

"Well, you're hitting a pretty good average."

"Yeah, I guess so. But I never look at the averages."

"You don't know you're leading the league?" asked the writer incredulously.

"Well, I hear people talking about it, but I don't pay much attention to what they say."

"And you never sneak a look at the batting averages?"

"No. I let my wife keep track of those things, and we never talk about it."

"I don't get it, Willie," said the writer. "Isn't it important to you?"

"Well, not *that* important. I just go up there and try to do the best I can every day. Then I forget about it. There's one thing more important to me than my batting average."

"What's that?"

"Winning. When the team wins, that's what counts."

"What about the All-Star team?" pursued the writer. "Think you'll make it?"

"I really haven't thought much about it," said Willie. "I know it would be an honor to play on it, but I'm not figuring on it. Right now my wife and I are planning to take a trip east in the three days we have off during the All-Star Game."

"You might not have them off," mumbled the writer as he walked away.

It was now June 15 and the Tigers were in Boston to play the Red Sox. The game turned out to be one of those cliff-hangers where the lead changes continuously.

Boston leaped on the Tigers for three runs in the top of the first inning, and it looked as if the Detroiters were in for a tough night. But the Tigers roared back for two in the bottom of the fourth, only to see the Red Sox grab two more in the sixth to make the score Boston 5, Detroit 2.

That lead lasted until the Tigers came to bat in the last of the eighth. Arnold Early was pitching for Boston, and he got off to a bad start by hitting shortstop Dick McAuliffe with a pitch. Jerry Lumpe then rapped a double to right field and McAuliffe pulled up at third. Gates Brown singled and McAuliffe scored to make the count Boston 5, Detroit 3.

With Kaline and Horton coming up, and two men on the bags, Boston manager Billy Herman took out Early and substituted the fire-balling Dick Radatz. Radatz was known around the league as The Monster—a guy who could fire a ball so fast that it was almost invisible.

Kaline found him unhittable and popped up. That brought up Willie the Wonder.

Horton waved his bat at Radatz. The Monster toed the rubber and fired a ball outside.

"Ball one!"

Horton waited motionlessly. Radatz delivered again. In tight, on the corner. One-and-one.

The count climbed to two-and-one, then three-and-one. Radatz reared back and blazed a fast ball over for strike two.

The count was full.

Radatz toed the rubber again. His arms went up, came down, the pitch was on its way. Willie swung at the blur. There was a loud crack and the blur climbed high and far into left center field. It cleared the wall and landed in the seats for a home run, finishing off a four-run rally and putting the Tigers ahead, 6–5. That's the way the game ended.

After the game Horton was talking to the usual number of reporters around his locker. Never quite willing to give himself full credit for his accomplishments, he explained the home run in negative fashion.

"It's kind of funny," he said. "But Radatz's pitch wasn't really a good one. He'd been feeding them to me low and outside but this one was inside and high—right under my chin. Guess I shouldn't have even swung at it. I didn't get the fat part of the bat on it, I just hit it on the handle."

Gates Brown always chuckled over such explanations.

"Wonder what'll happen if he ever gets some *good* wood on the ball?" he asked.

Chapter 9

During the last couple of weeks in June, Willie Horton continued his savage assault on American League pitchers. On June 16 he was instrumental in bringing home a Tiger victory over Boston by hitting a double in the seventh inning with two men on and the score 4–3 in favor of the Red Sox. Then, in the eighth, he hit one of the longest home runs of his career, a tremendous drive deep into the center field stands. The Tigers won, 9–4.

That was when the Detroit newspaper began to wonder out loud whether Willie might win the triple crown. He was leading the league in home runs with 15. He had the highest batting average with .363. And he had 46 RBIs.

A few days later, Detroit and Kansas City tangled in a slugging match that featured some sensational moments for the Tigers. The Athletics jumped on the Tigers for six runs in the first inning and added two more in the second to take an 8–0 lead. That looked like the ball game right there. But in the last half of the second Detroit got going. Willie Horton lashed his sixteenth homer of the season into the upper deck in left field, and first baseman Norm Cash hit another one to make the score Kansas City 8, Detroit 2.

After that it was all Tigers. They scored four in the third and two in the fourth to tie it up at 8-all, then slugged their way to four more in the fifth to make it 12–8. That was the final score. It was an inspiring victory and it put Detroit only three games out of first place.

With a sensational season in the making, Willie Horton began to learn what success meant. Newspapers and magazines were eager for stories about him. He was requested to make public appearances. Everybody in Detroit—and, indeed, in other American League cities—was talking about the big slugger. Dressen was particularly vocal.

"He's got what it takes and the sky is the limit for him," he said. "Why, Willie's so strong that he can be fooled on a pitch and still hit it 400 feet. One of the big differences this year is that he's hitting the breaking pitches to right field. Before, he was trying to pull everything to left."

Horton was, in fact, the most spectacular and exciting player the Tigers had had since the days of Hank Greenberg in the thirties and forties. The only two players since Greenberg who might have qualified as exciting players were Al Kaline and Rocky Colavito. But Kaline, despite his great skills, was never explosive, and Colavito simply never caught on in Detroit as he had at Cleveland.

But here was Willie Horton, a hometown boy who could hit a ball to kingdom come, a player who could break up a pitchers' battle with one swing of the bat—and all Detroit loved him. He was well on the way to becoming the idol of half the population, but none of this went to Willie's head. In fact, he paid very little attention to it.

What Horton was striving for, more than anything else, was perfection. His aim was to become the perfect ballplayer, and if that made him a gate attraction and a Detroit hero—well, okay. But he never thought in terms of being a hero. In fact, even the money wasn't important—at least, not all-inclusively important. He didn't know, exactly, what his take-home pay was. The Tigers sent his check on payday to Damon Keith, the Detroit lawyer who had been his legal guardian until he reached the age of twenty-one. Keith put some of it in the bank and doled the rest out to Mrs. Horton to run the house. Both Willie and his wife preferred it that way.

And unlike most ballplayers, Willie rarely read what was written about him. The newspapers lauding his feats held no charm for him.

"I never pay much attention to what the newspapers are saying about me," he said one day. "I leave all that to my wife. She's keeping all the clippings in a scrapbook."

One reporter grinned at him and said, "What are you batting, Willie?"

Willie grinned right back. "Gee, I don't know. I guess I'm doing all right though."

On June 30 another honor came to Horton. He was chosen by the players of the league for the All-Star Game. Earl Battey of the Minnesota Twins topped the voting with 202 votes, but Willie Horton was right behind with 198, winning out over established stars such as Carl Yastrzemski, Leon Wagner and Mickey Mantle.

"I'm glad to make the team," he said proudly. "It's an honor. But I never expected to make it. I thought I'd spend three days with my family instead."

By July 4 the Tigers had reached what appeared to be their level. They were in fifth place with 42 wins and 34 losses. Cleveland and Minnesota were tied for first place, the Chicago White Sox trailed them by three games, Baltimore was four and a half back and Detroit was five behind.

Despite all the excitement being created by Willie the Wonder, the Tigers were not excelling as a team.

On July 9 Horton had himself a day at the expense of the Athletics in Kansas City. Fred Talbot was pitching for the A's and the Kansas City crowd booed Willie when he stepped to the plate for his first turn at bat—a form of recognition reserved for players who scare their opponents half to death. Horton hit one of Talbot's slants so hard that Joe McGuff, baseball writer for the *Kansas City Star,* called it the longest home run ever hit in Municipal Stadium.

There was a nine-mile-an-hour gale blowing in from center field when he hit the ball, but Willie sent it screaming to left center, bucking the wind all the way. The ball traveled over the 408-foot mark in deep left center, cleared a wall 10 feet high, an auxiliary scoreboard 8 feet high and a back wall 25 feet away. It was his twentieth homer of the season and the twelfth that had traveled 400 feet or better.

"That," said Norm Cash in the locker room, "ought to get you ready for the All-Star Game."

The All-Star contest was played on July 12, and the National League defeated the American League, 6–5. Horton batted three times and failed to hit, but this failure didn't bother him. He was thrilled at being able to play with the best men in the game, and he was particularly proud of the fact that he was the only player permitted to play the full nine innings.

The Tigers were still in fifth place when the season resumed, but they were now seven games behind the league-leading Minnesota Twins. The Tigers had been slipping a little before the All-Star break, and now they faced a make-or-break schedule. There were only two soft touches coming up in their next twenty-seven games; the Tigers had four to play with Boston, five with Cleveland, seven with New York, nine with Chicago and two with Washington.

"If we do well in the next twenty-seven games," said Dressen, "we'll be in the running. If we don't, things will be tough."

The Tigers started out badly. They lost three of the first four games, with all the hitters slumping at the same time. That included Willie Horton, who had 2-for-19.

The Tigers returned home on July 20 to play the only soft touch of the twenty-seven-game test, the Washington Senators. The game was a pitchers' duel, but it was settled in the fourth inning when Kaline walked with two out and Horton drilled a tape-measure homer into the left field stands off Howie Koplitz. It was his twenty-first.

On July 23 the Tigers and the White Sox tangled in a four-game series with fourth place at stake. Chicago was six and a half games behind the leading Minnesota Twins, and the Tigers were seven games out. The Tigers therefore had an excellent chance to pass Chicago in the standings.

The first game of the series started out grimly for both Willie Horton and the Tigers. In the third inning with a runner on base, Chicago's Pete Ward slashed a drive to left field. Horton started in on the ball, then realized he had misjudged it and that it would carry over his head. He backpedaled furiously, but he could not catch up to the drive and the ball went over his head for a double that scored a run.

By the time the sixth inning came around, Chicago held a 4–2 lead. Horton was the first man up and he was anxious to redeem himself. He did by slashing a double to left center. It sparked a three-run rally. Shortstop Dick McAuliffe singled Horton home, catcher Bill Freehan hit a homer and the Tigers went on to win the game, 6–5. The victory moved the Tigers into fourth place, ahead of the White Sox.

The next night the Tigers won, 7–4, and strengthened their hold on fourth place. It was their fifth straight victory. Then, rubbing salt into the White Sox wounds, the Tigers took both ends of a doubleheader the following day, 10–6 and 13–2.

But just when things were looking up, the Tigers lapsed into a batting slump again, and by the end of July they were still seven and a half games behind Minnesota.

August turned out to be a frustrating month for Detroit. Injuries began to riddle the team. Kaline was in and out of the lineup with bruised ribs, and shortstop Dick McAuliffe suffered a broken hand. Still, the Tigers managed to win a fair share of games. The only trouble was, Minnesota was winning almost all of theirs and gradually stretching their lead over the rest of the American League teams.

It was on August 8, when the Yanks defeated the Tigers 6–5, that the players began to realize that the pennant was slipping away. They were now eleven and a half games behind the front-running Twins, and catching up seemed an impossibility.

"We're in trouble," admitted pitcher Hank Aguirre. "The Twins just never lose."

The other players expressed similar views. Even Horton was sagging at the plate, and he worried about his ineffectiveness.

"I don't think I'm doing anything wrong," he said. "I'm doing the same things up there, but the hits just aren't falling in for me."

Manager Charlie Dressen was particularly aware of this fact, and on August 10, in a game against Kansas City, Horton found himself benched. In his place was his friend and roomie, Gates Brown. Horton, who always had a fine sense of loyalty to anyone befriending him, slapped Brown on the back.

"Go get 'em, Gates," he said.

Gates got 'em, all right. He singled in the Tigers' first run. Then he made a long run from left to center to snag a fly. And later on he got a single. Detroit won the game, 3–0.

Horton cheered him in the dugout during the game. When a

sportswriter commented about it later, Horton shrugged. "We're good friends," he said simply. "I like to see Gates do well. It'll always be like that between us. No matter what happens on the field, we'll always be friends off the field."

The reign of Gates Brown lasted only one night. Horton was back in the left field the following night and slammed a home run off Rollie Sheldon, his twenty-third, to help whip Kansas City, 6–2. The next day the Tigers won, 11–1, and seemed to be definitely out of their hitting slump.

Just before the middle of August a change was made in the Tiger lineup. Dressen talked to Willie in the dugout before the game.

"Kaline's come up with a sore foot," he said. "As long as he's out, I'd like to play Gates in the outfield. Think you could switch to right field and let Gates play left?"

Horton nodded. "Anything you say. If you think it will help the team, it's okay with me."

So in a doubleheader with the Los Angeles Angels, Horton played right field. The Tigers won both games, 9–2 and 9–5, and Horton found no difficulty in playing the strange position. The two wins moved the Tigers into a tie with the Cleveland Indians for second place, although they were still eight games behind the leading Twins. Gates Brown, on a hitting rampage, had two singles, two doubles and a home run. Horton had to be satisfied with one double, but it drove in two runs and pushed his RBIs up to 77.

Minnesota was the next team to move into the Tigers' lair for a three-game series. Since the Twins led by eight games, it could hardly be called a crucial series, but one reporter described it as a "somewhat crucial" series, which seemed to fit the facts more accurately.

Kaline was ready to play again, although he was hobbling, and Dressen put him in center field with Horton and Gates Brown flanking him. And in the first game the Tigers went on a home run spree. They hit four homers, and Horton had two of them. One was a leadoff home run into the lower deck in left field off Dave Boswell; the other was hit with Don Demeter and Al Kaline on base. The score was Detroit 7, Minnesota 4, and Horton had driven in four of the seven runs.

That cut the Twins' lead to seven games, but in the next two contests the Tigers looked flat, losing them both and falling nine games off the pace.

In late August and early September more Tigers suffered injuries. Don Demeter broke his left wrist, pitcher Denny McLain was laid up with a virus, and assorted injuries caused shortstop Ray Oyler, infielder Jake Wood, outfielder Mickey Stanley and Gates Brown to miss games. During this trying time, Willie Horton played well, on one occasion rapping his twenty-seventh home run against Washington to take the league lead, and driving in three runs to make his total 91, one behind Rocky Colavito.

The next day Horton knocked in two more runs and tied Rocky at 93 RBIs.

But Horton didn't escape the injury jinx entirely. On September 7 he injured his left heel and was taken to the hospital. He missed three games, but that's all he could stand. Despite soreness in the heel, he went to Dressen in the clubhouse.

"I'm ready to play," he said.

"Are you sure?" Dressen asked cagily.

"I'm sure. You put me in there and I'll show you some hitting in the last three weeks of the season."

At this point, Horton had 93 RBIs with 18 games to go, and suddenly he had a new ambition.

"I want to be the first Tiger in two years to drive in a hundred runs," he said.

"How do you know you'd be the first Tiger in two years to

drive in a hundred runs?" asked a writer. "I thought you never looked at statistics."

Horton looked sheepish. "Somebody told me," he said.

Anyway, Horton got his wish. By the end of the season he had accumulated 104 runs-batted-in. And on the last day of the season the Tigers clinched fourth place with two wins over Washington. Their record was only four games better than their previous year, but the Tigers were laying the foundation for a better team.

When the sixty-seven-year-old Dressen received another one-year contract toward the end of the season, he said, "We'll have an improved team next year. We're looking for our young players to come through, and Kaline, who was hurting a lot this year, should be back in shape after he has an operation this winter on his foot."

"And Willie Horton?" asked a reporter.

"Don't worry about Willie," said Dressen. "He'll be better, too."

As a matter of fact, Willie Horton had done extremely well during 1965. He had hit 29 home runs, 14 of which traveled 400 feet or more. He had 104 RBIs, second highest total in the American League. His batting average was .273, and he had established himself as the No. 1 batting threat on the Tiger team.

Willie Horton completed his first full season with Detroit highly pleased with his performance. Only one thing disappointed him. The Tigers had finished 13 games behind the pennant-winning Minnesota Twins.

Chapter 10

Willie Horton's sudden emergence as a full-fledged baseball star had little influence on the way he looked at life. Although he was now established in a lucrative profession and had more money than he had ever dreamed possible, he did not forget his beginnings. He still remembered the hungry days in the ghettos of Detroit, when his family was able to eke out only a bare subsistence, and particularly he remembered the kids on the street corners and the temptation to make trouble that always brewed among them. Willie had been one of those kids.

He felt, now that his name was well known in Detroit, that he could use it to encourage children of his race to make something of their lives. One day he said to a reporter, "You know, I worry about the kids that live down where I used to live. I was lucky. I happened to be able to play baseball pretty well, and I thank God to this day that he gave me the talent that I have. But some of those kids don't have this talent, and with nothing to occupy their minds they'll get into trouble. I feel I have an obligation to try to keep them out of trouble."

Horton didn't just talk about it. He took action. He would go down into the slums of Detroit, walk around the old neighborhoods and talk to kids on the street corners. When he approached them, he'd say, "I'm Willie Horton," and that would open their eyes wide. Everyone knew Willie Horton, the kids on the corner especially, and they would listen to him as he talked, as he encouraged them to do something constructive with their lives, to get part-time jobs after school, to make proper use of their leisure time.

On other occasions, he would go back to Northwestern High School, where his name was legendary as a school athlete, and talk to groups of growing young boys. Often Damon Keith would go with him, or he would meet with his old high school coach, Sam Bishop. And he was always welcome wherever he went, not because he was Willie Horton of the Tigers, but for the good he was doing.

Patricia Horton sometimes worried about her husband's inclination to go into some of the worst neighborhoods to talk to youngsters.

"I'm afraid of what might happen," she told him many times. "It's a rough neighborhood and some hoodlums might go for you."

Horton recognized the danger. "Sometimes I'm afraid, too," he admitted, "but I feel it's something I have to do."

Much of Willie Horton's time, during the winter of 1965–66, was spent in good work among the underprivileged children of the city of Detroit. And then, quite suddenly, it was time for him to go down to Lakeland, Florida, for 1966 spring training with the Tigers.

Willie, of course, knew he had had a good season with the Tigers, but he was taking nothing for granted. In fact, he and Gates Brown drove down to Florida a week early.

"I want to get a good start," Horton explained. "You can't rest on what you did last year. I want to improve my hitting for *this* year."

In the quiet atmosphere of a training camp that had not yet officially opened, Willie Horton stood in the batter's box and hit against the pitching machine until he raised blisters on his hands. Then he continued to hit until the blisters bled.

"Maybe you'd better quit," said Brown, looking at Horton's raw hands.

"Yeah," agreed Willie. "But at least I've got my timing."

When the rigors of spring training were over and the exhibition games came along, the Tigers moved into a spanking new ball park called Marchant Stadium. It was a beautiful park with "major league" written all over it, and it was a credit to both the Tigers and the city of Lakeland.

During the Grapefruit League games the Tigers played only .500 ball, but this was hardly a measure of their strength. They experimented continually with rookies, and on very few occasions did they present a really strong starting lineup. They knew what their veterans could do, and the job was to find the young men coming up the ladder to make the team stronger.

Willie, of course, was one of those young men, and his performance was spectacular. One incident occurred during a game that had the whole team talking.

Horton was at the plate and umpire Hank Soar was behind it, calling balls and strikes. The pitcher stretched and delivered a sizzling fast ball. Horton swung viciously at the ball and missed it. But as he swung the fat end of the bat broke off and went sailing halfway out to the pitcher's mound. Willie had the handle still in his hand.

After the game Hank Soar was shaking his head in the clubhouse.

"How do you like that?" he said in amazement. "He didn't even make contact with the ball, but so help me, the big end of the bat broke off when he stopped his swing, he swung with such force!"

Willie just smiled. In his habitual way of playing down anything complimentary to him, he said, "I fouled off the pitch before that. Maybe the bat cracked a little."

Pat Mullin, the Tiger first base coach, laughed. "Maybe so," he said, "but it's still a pretty good stunt!"

As the Tigers headed north to begin the regular season, baseball men were expressing cautious optimism about their chances. Most of the experts thought the Tigers would finish in fourth place, although a few placed them third or even second. One reason for this appraisal was the fact that the Tigers had added Bill Monbouquette to their pitching staff. He had been obtained from the Boston Red Sox in exchange for infielder George Smith and outfielder George Thomas. Another reason for rating the Tigers highly was that they had three "kid pitchers"—Denny McLain, Joe Sparma and Mickey Lolich—who were expected to perform great feats of wizardry on the mound.

"That's a real pitching staff," said one Tiger supporter. "Those three kids have the best young arms in the league, and with the experienced Monbo on the staff, they're going to be hard to beat."

In addition to the great things expected of the pitching staff, the Tigers had an outfield that was rated as the most talented in the league. The incomparable Al Kaline was in right field, speedy ballhawk Mickey Stanley in center, and slugging Willie Horton in left. The infield was also a reasonably steady one with Don Wert at third base, Dick McAuliffe at short, Jerry Lumpe at second and Norm Cash at first. Bill Freehan was behind the plate. When the Tigers opened their season on April 12 against the Yankees at New York, Mickey Lolich was elected to pitch the first game.

The Tigers got away to a fast start by winning the opener, 2–1, on a fine pitching performance by Lolich. Then they took the next two games from the Yankees, 3–2 and 5–2, on good pitching by Denny McLain and Monbouquette. With three wins and no losses, the Tigers came back to Detroit to open their home season against the Washington Senators.

Willie Horton had not been exactly a ball of fire in the first three games, but Washington's pitcher, Pete Richert, seemed to appeal to him. In the first inning Don Wert opened with a single and promptly stole second. Jerry Lumpe fanned, but Norm Cash ripped a single to right. Wert, trying to score, was out at the plate. Then Al Kaline walked.

That put two men on as Willie Horton strode to the plate. Horton went through his ritual of stepping into the batter's box —and it had become just that with Horton, a ritual. He stepped in with his left foot, then his right, twisted his right toe into the ground, never looking at the pitcher, ignoring him as if he didn't exist. Then he tapped the far side of the plate with his bat, to make sure the swing of the bat would cover the entire area of the plate, then took a couple of practice swings and *then* faced the pitcher.

"They were quick pitching me last year, before I had my mind made up," said Willie one time. "So this year I'm taking my time getting set."

Willie was set this time. He hit Richert's first pitch 400 feet into left center for his first home run of the new season. It scored three runs and the Tigers went on to win, 7–5, for their fourth straight victory.

The next day the Tigers lost their first game and things began to slip a little. By April 23 they had six wins and four losses and nobody on the team was hitting. That included Horton, who, despite the home run against Washington, was looking pitiful at the plate.

"We haven't jelled yet," was Dressen's comment, a statement vague enough to mean anything.

Horton's personal slump continued. On April 24, in a doubleheader, he was up eight times and got only one hit. The next few days were just as bad, and finally Dressen benched him.

"I've got to try something to shake the club up," he said. "I'm going with Jim Northrup in left field."

Despite his disappointment, Horton saw the realism in Dressen's thinking.

"If it will help the club, that's what you have to do," he told Dressen.

Northrup responded to his opportunity with a home run that day. And Willie thought, *that's what I've got to do if I want to stay in there.*

By May 1 the Tigers were in fourth place. The Baltimore Orioles, off to a raging start, were in first place with 12 wins and 1 loss. The Cleveland Indians, almost as good, were second with 11–1. Then came the Chicago White Sox with 10–4 and the Detroit Tigers with 10–7.

During this frustrating period Horton was in and out of the lineup as Dressen juggled his players in an attempt to come up with a winning combination. Willie was having his troubles, and like all players when they're in a hitting slump, he didn't know why. He was hitting only .160 and in one sequence he had managed only 2 hits in 31 times at bat. Horton worried himself to sleep every night. He thought, *if I don't do better than this, I'll be out of the lineup for good!*

On May 10 the Tigers were in Cleveland to play the Indians. Horton was on the bench again, and the Tiger outfield consisted of Kaline, Brown and Northrup. It was a low-score game, and when Detroit came to bat in the top of the ninth the teams were deadlocked at two runs each. Bill Freehan was leadoff man for the Tigers, and he dropped a blooper single into left field. Mickey

Lolich, who had pitched a fine game, was lifted for a pinch hitter. The pinch hitter was Horton.

Willie responded by tagging a fast ball and driving it to right field. It smashed against the fence and scored Freehan with what proved to be the winning run.

Horton was happy in the clubhouse that day. It was the first important hit he'd had in a long time. A writer, talking to Willie, said, "I just heard a remark in the Cleveland clubhouse that that was the first hit you'd had to right field since you were fourteen years old."

The remark had been made by Birdie Tebbetts, manager of the Indians. Horton looked up at the writer. "Who said that?" he wanted to know.

"Birdie Tebbetts," said the writer.

"Who's he?" asked Horton.

Again, it was an honest question. Names and reputations always eluded Horton; he had no memory for them.

"Tebbetts happens to be the Cleveland manager," said the writer.

"Oh," was Horton's comment.

It was not until May 15 that Willie Horton really roared out of his long slump. The Tigers were playing the Chicago White Sox in Detroit, and Tommy John was the Chicago starting pitcher. In the first inning, Don Wert and Jerry Lumpe were easy outs, but with two away the fireworks exploded. Norm Cash ripped a single to right, Kaline hit a single to center and Don Demeter rapped another to right, scoring Cash. One run in, two out and two men on base. And Willie Horton up.

On the mound, Tommy John studied Horton with the curiosity of a robin regarding a worm. He knew that Horton had not been hitting, but he also knew Willie's capabilities. He could take no chances.

John hit the outside corner for a strike that Willie let go by.

The next ball was in tight, backing Horton away. Horton swung like a rusty gate at the next pitch and missed.

One ball, two strikes.

Horton backed out of the batter's box, got dirt on his hands and moved back in. He cocked his bat over his right shoulder and waited. Tommy John reared back, his leg went up, the pitch came in.

Horton swung and there was the sharp crack of bat meeting ball. The ball soared into left center, bounced between the converging outfielders and bounded to the fence. Two runs raced across the plate and Willie came to a halt on third base with a triple.

It put the Tigers ahead, 3–0.

Chicago, however, refused to roll over and play dead. In the second inning they put together three runs of their own to tie the game.

In the fourth the Tigers tried some daring strategy in an effort to go ahead again. Al Kaline, with one out, singled. Willie singled for his second hit of the game, sending Kaline to third. Freehan was ordered to try the suicide squeeze—a play in which the batter bunts the ball at the same time the runner on third comes racing into the plate. If it's done right, the runner can score easily; if the batter misses the ball, however, the runner coming into the plate is too far committed to return to third and is an easy out.

In this case, Freehan missed. Kaline, almost on top of the plate, was tagged out, and then the ball was thrown to second in time to nail Horton going from first to second.

Chicago went ahead 4–3 in the fifth, but the Tigers scored three times in the seventh to take a lead that lasted. The final score was Detroit 8, Chicago 6, and Willie added a double to his collection of hits for the day.

"A single, double and triple," said Horton with satisfaction. "That's better. That's much better."

On May 16, tragedy hit the Detroit club again. The Tigers were taking batting practice in preparation for a midseason exhibition game with the St. Louis Cardinals. Suddenly Jim Campbell, Tiger general manager, appeared on the dugout steps and waved the team into the clubhouse. Campbell appeared nervous and unstrung. His face was pale.

"What now?" Horton mumbled to Kaline.

"The way things have been going, it could be anything."

In hushed tones Campbell announced that Charlie Dressen was ill again and had been rushed to Henry Ford Hospital.

"I can't tell you how serious it is yet," he said. "We just don't know. But we know he won't be back for a while. Bob Swift will take over managership of the team during Charlie's absence."

The Tigers filed out onto the field in a renewed state of shock. There were no longer dissidents on the Tiger team where Charlie Dressen was concerned. The fireball manager had won over every player on the club.

Of all the players on the team, probably Horton was the hardest hit. He felt suddenly as if all the pep and enthusiasm had gone out of him. His respect for the little manager was a soaring one.

"It's terrible," he said. "I feel all drained out."

The Tigers went through the motions of playing the Cardinals in a semitrance. By the next evening, as they prepared to play the New York Yankees at Tiger Stadium, they had heard the worst. Charlie Dressen had suffered his second heart attack in fourteen months, and there were rumors that the peppery little manager would never again return to the game.

In the clubhouse before the Tigers took the field against the Yanks, acting manager Bob Swift held a short meeting. His voice was grave.

"Nobody knows when Charlie will be back, if he ever will,"

he said. "Meantime, you know how I operate. My rules are the same as Charlie's. Let's go out and win one for Charlie."

The Tigers beat New York 7–2 that night, with Horton contributing a home run off pitcher Dooley Womack, who had completed his prior six relief appearances without allowing a run.

"It sure felt good," was Horton's comment.

But consistency was not a Horton distinction, and at this point Willie went back into a slump again. But even with Charlie's absence and Willie's ineffectiveness, the Tigers still did well. On May 21 they whipped Baltimore, 7–5, and this victory moved them into second place, only two games behind the league-leading Cleveland Indians.

Sometimes, when a player slumps at bat, his fielding also suffers. In Horton's case, however, this didn't happen. He continued to field his position well, and on May 22, in a game against Baltimore, he exhibited his competency in the field dramatically.

The Tigers were leading Baltimore, 3–2, in the ninth when the Orioles started a rally. Frank Robinson doubled off Mickey Lolich and Swift immediately brought in Larry Sherry in relief. Brooks Robinson smacked Sherry's first pitch into left field for a single—the kind of hit that should have scored Frank Robinson from second.

Robinson wheeled around third and headed for the plate with the tying run. In left field, Willie came in fast on the hit, scooped it up in his glove on the first bounce and, in the same motion, uncorked a throw to Bill Freehan at the plate. The ball traveled like a bullet, took one skip into Freehan's big mitt, and the surprised Robinson was out at the plate.

But Horton's long batting slump continued, and during the last two weeks of May, Swift began thinking about playing Jim Northrup in left field and holding out Horton for pinch-hitting roles. The Tigers were in third place, four and a half games behind the leading Indians, and were very much in the race. Swift had to juggle his players until he found a winning lineup.

"Maybe," Swift said, "a rest will help you."

Horton nodded. He was not convinced that a rest would help at all, and he hated the thought of sitting on the bench. But he took Swift's decision without complaint.

"If you think it will help the team," he said, "it's okay with me."

Chapter 11

Jim Northrup replaced Willie Horton in most of the games for the balance of the month, and on a few occasions when Horton was reinstated in the lineup he went hitless. On June 3 Swift wrote Horton's name in the lineup when the team played the California Angels at Anaheim. Willie, at that time, had failed to hit in his last 29 times at bat.

The game turned out to be a battle between pitchers, and at the end of six innings the score was 0–0. Horton had been handcuffed all night by California pitcher Marcelino Lopez, and he was the picture of frustration as he paced the dugout before the seventh inning started. Finally he turned to Mickey Stanley.

"Mickey, can I use your bat?" he asked.

"Sure."

"I hope there's a hit in it for me," Willie said. "There haven't been many in mine lately."

Horton took Stanley's bat and walked to the plate. Marcelino Lopez peered in at the hulky Horton and fired a fast ball inside.

"Ball one!"

The next pitch came in over the heart of the plate and Horton stood there transfixed.

"Stuh-rike!"

With the count one-and-one, Lopez delivered a pitch inside and low that the umpire would have called a ball. But Willie swung and golfed the ball into center field. Miraculously, the ball continued to rise until it carried over the fence at the 400-foot mark!

It won the game for the Tigers, 1–0, and Horton was as happy as if he had gone five-for-five.

"It's about time I did something for the club," he said. "I think I'll keep on using Stanley's bat."

"Oh, no you don't!" objected Stanley. "You'll use up all the base hits in it and there won't be any left for me!"

"Willie was going to right with outside pitches for a while," said Swift analytically, "but lately he fell into the habit of trying to pull everything. We've been trying to tell Willie to meet the ball where it is pitched—and he met this one low and inside."

In the California clubhouse nobody appreciated Horton's feat. Lopez, the losing pitcher, shook his head slowly. "Nobody—but nobody—can hit a low inside pitch that far!" he said. And then he added, "Nobody, I guess, but Horton."

The next day some good news came to the Tigers for a change. Charlie Dressen had improved enough to be released from the hospital. He was quartered in a suite at the Sheraton-Cadillac Hotel in Detroit, and there was now conjecture that he might return to the game soon.

"The doctors will have the final word as to if, or when, he can return to baseball," Campbell said.

No one was happier than Horton to hear the news. The Tigers had returned to Tiger Stadium to meet the Boston Red Sox, and Willie seemed inspired by the good report on Dressen. He had three hits in three times up, and the last of the three hits was a rousing triple to the right center field wall. He scored on a fly by Bill Freehan, and that proved to be the winning run in a close 2–1 Tiger victory.

And the victory moved them to within one game of the league lead.

The Tigers won five in a row then, but failed to gain on the high-flying Baltimore Orioles. By June 11, when the New York Yankees ended their winning streak, they were one and a half games out.

Still, the Tigers were very much in the running and with the first pennant in twenty-one years beckoning them, Tiger management went all-out to make a trade that would salt away the flag. On June 14 they traded Don Demeter to the Boston Red Sox for pitcher Earl Wilson. The feeling was that the Tigers enjoyed enough fine outfielders and could afford to part with Demeter to add strength to their pitching staff.

When Wilson arrived, Swift called Horton over. "You two guys are going to be roomies on the road," he said flatly.

Horton and Wilson looked at each other.

"I guess we're going to have to be friends," Wilson said. He was remembering the confrontation they had had when he had decked Willie with an inside pitch and Willie had threatened to come out and "move him like a mountain."

Horton grinned. "That's okay with me," he said, and the two shook hands.

Although the Tigers were in the thick of the pennant race, the fans were not yet becoming unduly excited. The Tigers had been tagged as "pennant threats" for so many years, with no pennant materializing, that the fans were in a show-me frame of mind. They were content to sit back and wait, to find out if this team was for real.

On June 16 the Tigers blasted the Boston Red Sox, 16–4, and Horton had a home run and two singles and drove in six runs. As usual, he wasn't particularly aware of his feat. In the clubhouse a reporter said, "Did you ever drive in six runs in a game before?"

Horton looked up in surprise. "Is that how many I had?"

"Sure. Don't you count them?"

Horton shook his head. "Naw. I'll let you do that."

It seemed that Willie Horton had finally emerged from his long batting slump. He was whacking the ball like the Horton of old, and the ball was dropping in for him—quite often, into the stands. When the team arrived in Yankee Stadium on June 18 to play the Bronx Bombers, Horton was in a happy frame of mind.

"I think we're going to move now," he predicted.

The Yankees tossed Al Downing at the Tigers in an effort to keep them from moving. In the first inning he disposed of the first two Tiger batters handily, but Norm Cash singled to right and Kaline walked to put two men on with two out and Horton up.

Downing fired the ball outside. Ball. The next pitch was ball two, and Downing had to come in with one. Horton swung, the ball headed like a shot from a cannon into center field, and Cash raced home with the first run of the game.

The 1–0 lead held until the Yankee fourth when Roger Maris tied the score with a long fly into the right field seats. In the fifth the Yankees scored another when Tom Tresh hit a homer. Score: Yankees 2, Tigers 1.

Battling back, the Tigers rallied in the sixth. Cash opened the inning with a single. Kaline fanned. Horton then rapped another single into left, with Cash pulling up at second. Northrup singled Cash home and sent Willie the Wonder to third. He scored on another single by Bill Freehan.

The Tigers were now ahead, 3–2.

This lead didn't last long either. The Yanks put together a walk, single and a sacrifice fly to score a run and deadlock the count at 3–3, and the tie endured until the Tigers came to bat in the top of the eighth.

Pedro Ramos was now pitching for New York, and the first man he faced in the top of the eighth was Willie Horton. Ramos tried to get a fast ball by Horton and found out he couldn't do it. Horton swung and lashed a drive down the third base line for a double. When Northrup flied to deep right center, Horton tagged up and went to third after the catch. Freehan singled him home and the score was 4–3 in favor of the Tigers.

That's the way it ended, with Willie having played a key part in each scoring inning.

A few days later the Tigers were playing the Senators in Washington and Phil Ortega was serving them up for the Nats. Dick McAuliffe, the Tiger leadoff man, slammed a high pitch into the right field stands to open the first inning. Dick Tracewski then bounced out, but Norm Cash ripped a double to left field. Al Kaline promptly singled Cash to third and forced Washington manager Gil Hodges to make a fateful decision. Jim Northrup was the next hitter and Hodges decided to walk him, loading the bases and setting the stage for a double play.

"Load the bases to bring up Horton?" gasped a fan in the stands. "That don't make no sense!"

As it turned out, the fan was right and the manager was wrong. Ortega fed Horton an outside pitch, then caught the inside corner with a curve. On the third pitch Horton connected. The ball sailed high over the center field wall for a grand slam home run. It was a blow that paralyzed the Senators for the rest of the game. The Tigers won 12–2.

In addition to his homer, Willie had three other hits—two singles and a foul that hit his kneecap. The next day the knee was swollen and sore, but Horton insisted on playing.

"You're sure it's all right?" asked Swift.

"Yeah. I'll tape it up and it'll be okay."

As it turned out, Horton didn't last long. He aggravated the knee with a slide into second base and had to retire from the game in the third inning.

There are many players who will refuse to play, or ask to be excused, if they are slightly ill or hurt. Horton, however, loved the game of baseball and it hurt him to sit on the bench.

"I'll be able to play," he told Swift the next day. "Just write down my name in that lineup."

This time Horton stuck. The Tigers romped to a 15–3 decision over California at Anaheim, and Horton hit his eighth home run of the season. After the game a writer raised an interesting question.

"Did you know, Willie, that of the eight homers you've hit this season, six were hit on the road?" he asked.

"Is that right?" Willie asked, for he paid little attention to such details.

"Do you have any explanation for it?" the writer pried.

"Well," said Horton, "I might be pressing a little at home. I think we all press at home. People expect so much of us and we could be trying too hard. You know, we haven't done too well at home, and if we're going to go anywhere, we'll have to get started in our own park."

Al Kaline was standing nearby and he looked down at Horton who was on a stool removing his socks. "Tell me something, Willie," he said. "Were you trying to hit a home run out there tonight?"

"Naw. I was just swinging."

Kaline smiled. He was the "elder statesman" of the Tigers, a proven star over a long number of years to whom the younger players looked for advice.

"Just remember that," he told Willie. "We've all got to try for singles. The fences look so close in Detroit we want to hit home runs. If we forget about that, we'll be a tougher team to beat."

They were words of wisdom and Horton appreciated them.

"Al has forgotten more about baseball than most of us have ever learned," he said with respect.

By the end of June the standings showed the Tigers still in the race. Baltimore was on top and the Tigers were in second place, four games behind. There was, however, a serious problem. Detroit's pitching was on the verge of collapse. There had been no complete game pitched by a starter in the last ten. The relief corps was worn out from too frequent appearances. And despite the fact that Willie Horton was again belting the ball and driving in important runs, victory was becoming a rarity. In thirteen games up to July 4, the Tigers lost nine, and when the fourth of July dawned they were seven games behind the leading Baltimore Orioles and fading fast.

The Tigers looked tired and listless. The pitching staff was a shambles, allowing 63 runs in 12 games. The team ran up a five-game losing streak after July 4 before finally edging Minnesota, 4–3. The victory was only a momentary respite, for the decline continued. Everything went wrong. Starting pitchers were pounded, relievers could not halt the hitting, the Tiger batters consistently failed in the clutch and a lot of small things went wrong too frequently—like Willie losing a ball in the lights and dropping it, thus losing another game.

Mercifully, the All-Star break occurred on July 12, at a time when the Tigers could use the three-day rest. This time Horton didn't make the team. The Tigers were represented by Norm Cash, Bill Freehan, Al Kaline, Dick McAuliffe and Denny McLain. The National League edged the American League, 2–1, at St. Louis.

On July 15 the team was at home, hoping to get started on a winning streak that would salvage some of their self-respect. But then the second blow of the year hit the Tigers. Acting manager Bob Swift suddenly fell ill and was rushed to Henry Ford Hospital with what was described as a "virus infection in the lining of his stomach," called gastroenteritis.

It was the first time in the history of major league baseball that a team had lost two managers by illness in a single season.

General manager Jim Campbell, his brow corrugated with worry, announced that Frank Skaff, third base coach for the Tigers and for many years a manager in the Tiger farm system, would pilot the team while Swift was recovering in the hospital and Dressen was recuperating in the hotel.

As if spurred by the ill luck, the Tigers responded to Frank Skaff with two wins over Baltimore. But then the team stumbled again. They lost a doubleheader to Cleveland, 7–3 and 15–2, and their big gun, Willie Horton, went 0-for-7.

The hard luck didn't stop. A few days later the Tigers lost Dick McAuliffe. Suffering from food poisoning, he was sent to join Swift in the hospital.

"Maybe we ought to just move the whole team to the hospital," said Skaff, discouraged.

Actually, Swift's illness and McAuliffe's poisoning were the culmination of a long series of mishaps that the Tigers had suffered since the middle of May. It was on May 4 that center fielder Mickey Stanley broke his hand. A day later Dressen suffered his second heart attack. Two days after that Mickey Lolich had to go into the Army Reserve and was lost to the team for a while. On June 2 Jerry Lumpe pulled a leg muscle that sidelined him for three weeks. The next day Don Wert came down with a bronchial infection that knocked him out for thirteen games. McAuliffe's food poisoning was expected to keep him out of the lineup for at least two weeks, and on June 19 Al Kaline pulled a muscle in his side and was benched.

On June 19, 20 and 21, playing with a badly weakened team,

the Tigers took three straight whippings at the hands of the Baltimore Orioles. That put them eleven and a half games behind. The Tigers played like automatons, with no spark and no drive. No one hit. The starting pitchers were atrocious and the relief corps shoddy. The three defeats were a continuation of a three-week period during which the Tigers used 82 pitchers in 25 games, an indication of how low the pitching staff had sunk.

On July 22, still in the doldrums, the Tigers were in Cleveland to meet the Indians. The Tigers were dressing in the clubhouse when Jim Campbell called an impromptu meeting. Horton was standing near Cash.

"What's up now, I wonder?" he asked fearfully.

"It must be serious—it always is lately," said Cash.

In a shocked voice, Campbell told the club that Bob Swift had more than a stomach disturbance. He was suffering from lung cancer. His return to the club was as doubtful as Charlie Dressen's, maybe more doubtful.

The Tigers took the field in a state of shock and remorse. This news seemed like the last straw. Everything was happening to the team; it was just not their year.

But they bounced back during the game to defeat Cleveland, 10–5. Later, talking to writers, Campbell said, "Having three managers in one season will have an effect on this club, no doubt about it. Whenever you change the atmosphere there is a feeling-out period until the ballplayers get to know just how the new man operates. Things are bound to be a little rough during times like this."

Not only was it tough adjusting to the ways of a new manager, but now rumors were sweeping the club. The big question was: Who would be the next Tiger manager? Most of the players, and the fans, now felt that neither Dressen nor Swift would ever return to the club. General manager Jim Campbell was in the awkward position of having to give thought to a new manager but at the same time not appear to do so until it was decided definitely by the doctors whether or not Charlie Dressen could return. Despite official silence on the subject, names cropped up in the newspapers—Billy Martin, the ex-Yankee and a Twins coach; Al Lopez, retired Chicago manager; and several others.

Chapter 12

The Tigers, still stubbornly insisting that they were not out of the race and could still win the pennant, were in Chicago to play the White Sox on July 26. It turned out to be a close and exciting game.

Chicago jumped off to a 1–0 lead in the third inning, but in the fourth the Tigers started trouble. Norm Cash walked to open the inning, and Horton stepped to the plate to test the slants of Joe Horlen. Horton didn't wait. The first pitch was to his liking and he clobbered it into the left field for a long double. Cash turned on the speed and scored from first base to tie the score, 1–1.

The tie held until the Tiger half of the sixth inning. Horlen was still on the mound and Al Kaline greeted him with a line single to center. Norm Cash topped a pitch and dribbled a grounder to the infield. There was no chance for a double play, but they nailed Cash at first as Kaline took second.

That brought up Horton again. Joe Horlen was more careful this time, trying to hit the corners with each pitch. He ran the count to 2-and-2, and then Horton swung at an outside pitch. The ball carried on a line over the first baseman's head for a single that scored Kaline.

That made the score 2–1 in favor of the Tigers.

In the eighth Hoyt Wilhelm, the knuckleballer, was on the mound for Chicago. He was a man that the greatest hitters in the game found difficult, but on this occasion Kaline sliced a double down the right field line to open the inning. Cash struck out, but on the third strike the knuckler got away from the Chicago catcher and Kaline raced to third.

For the third time in a crucial situation, Horton was at bat. Poised with the bat cocked over his shoulder, Willie waited for the inevitable knuckleball, since Wilhelm threw it almost exclusively. It came in, fluttering like a wounded butterfly, and Horton swung. He didn't connect solidly, but he got enough wood on the ball to propel it into center field. It dropped in for a hit and Kaline trotted home with the Tigers' third run.

The score at the end of the game was Tigers 3, White Sox 1, and Horton had collected four hits and driven in all three Tiger runs.

In the clubhouse later, Willie reflected on the blooper hit he had gotten in the eighth inning.

"The hits are starting to drop in for me now," he said. "It's not like it was earlier this year when everything was caught. You know, that must be the first hit I ever got off Wilhelm. But I'll take it."

It was a strange season. By August 1 the Tigers were still in second place, but they were fourteen and a half games behind the romping Baltimore Orioles. They could look back on the season and see exactly what had happened to them. On May 1 the Tigers had been only four games behind the Orioles. On June 1 they were five and a half back; on July 1 they were ten and a half; and on August 1 fourteen and a half. While the other clubs struggled, knocking each other off, the Baltimore Orioles were simply running away with the race.

And the Tigers, in second place, were actually closer to last place than they were to first!

Then, too, there seemed to be no end to the bad news where the Tigers were concerned. On August 5, with the Tigers on the road, news reached them that Charlie Dressen had been ordered back to the hospital, this time with a kidney infection. There was no indication, however, that his condition was at all serious. The Tigers drew a collective sigh and went to Boston for a doubleheader.

Horton, whose hits were falling in now, had a sensational day. In the first inning of the first game Don Wert led off for the Tigers with a homer. Dick Tracewski walked, Cash was out, and Kaline doubled. Horton doubled and Northrup tripled him home. That was four runs, all off pitching ace Jim Lonborg.

In the third Willie hit a home run and in the fifth he tripled to go 3-for-4 in the game. The Tigers won, 9–2.

The second game went against the Tigers, 7–6, but Horton contributed another home run and two singles to the Tiger attack. For the day he had collected six hits, driven in six runs, and hit two homers.

"A fair day's work, Willie," said Skaff.

"Like I say, they're falling in for me now."

Suddenly things began to look up for the Tigers, at least on the playing field. Encouraged, the Tigers traveled to Washington to meet the Senators at D.C. Stadium, and Mike McCormick took the hill for the Senators.

Both teams went down without a score in the opening inning, but in the Tiger half of the second Kaline shot a single to center field. Horton stepped into the box and waggled his bat at McCormick. McCormick looked in for his sign, caught the signal for a fast ball, stretched and shot the ball toward the plate. Willie swung and missed, almost falling down from the force of the cut he had taken. McCormick looked in again. The catcher signed for a slider. McCormick reared back and fired the ball.

Horton swung and immediately felt the shock of bat hitting ball as it traveled up his powerful arms. The ball shot on a low line to left field and got past outfielder Frank Howard before he could take two steps. Kaline came home and Horton pulled up at second with a double. Horton scored moments later on another double. Score: Tigers 2, Senators 0.

For seven innings the score remained the same, and in the eighth the Tigers picked up another run to make it 3–0. It looked like a sure victory for the Tigers, but in the ninth the Senators unexpectedly rallied for three runs to tie the score.

In the tenth Willie Horton had a chance to do something for the Tigers' cause but, batting against Bob Humphreys, he struck out. The third strike was a low fast ball inside, and Horton looked bad on it.

"He fooled me on it," Willie admitted in the dugout, "but he won't fool me again."

The tie endured through the eleventh inning and the Tigers came to bat in the twelfth. Dave Wickersham, the Tiger pitcher, was due to lead off the inning and Skaff sent in Jim Northrup to pinch-hit. Northrup topped one of Humphreys' pitches and dribbled a hit to the infield. Third baseman Don Wert was next up and Humphreys got him on strikes. Then Jake Wood went in to bat for Dick Tracewski and slapped a ball to short. But the Senator shortstop bobbled the ball and the Tigers had two men on and one out.

Horton fidgeted on the bench. He was eager to get up there and avenge himself against Humphreys for the strikeout, but there were two good men ahead of him—Norm Cash and Al Kaline. When Cash grounded out, the runners moved up to second and third, and Kaline stepped up to the plate determined to drive them home. But Gil Hodges, manager of the Senators, had other plans for Al. He signaled his pitcher to put Kaline on, thus creating a play at any base and bringing up Willie Horton.

Horton took his place at the plate. Humphreys went into his stretch and fired the ball. The umpire went up with his right hand.

"Stuh-rike!"

Humphreys got the ball back, peered in for the sign, nodded, then cut the outside edge with a curve.

"Stuh-rike!" barked the umpire.

Willie retreated from the box, nettled with himself for letting two pitches go by while he kept his bat on his shoulder. He got back in, took a practice cut, cocked the bat. The pitch came in, missing the outside corner.

Two strikes, one ball.

Horton had an idea what would be thrown next. A fast ball inside, the kind Humphreys had fanned him on before.

He was right. The ball came in, fast, inside, and Willie swung. This time he connected. The ball shot like a bullet into left field and fell in front of Frank Howard. Two runs came in on the single and the Tigers won, 5–3.

In the clubhouse Willie had an expansive smile pasted on his face.

"It was that low inside fast ball," he said. "He made me look bad on the same kind of pitch before. I made up my mind to hit that ball somewhere if he tried it again."

Willie Horton, who was now hitting like Willie Horton, put on another stellar exhibition the next day. For six innings the game was a tight pitchers' battle. Young Frank Kreutzer, virtually an unknown, held the Tigers scoreless, and when they came up in the sixth the score was Washington 1, Detroit 0.

It looked as if the Tigers would never be able to solve Kreutzer's baffling assortment of pitches, because both Don Wert and Jerry Lumpe were easy outs. But Cash and Kaline both walked, and

Horton, leveling on Kreutzer's first pitch, tied the score, 1–1, with a sharp single to left.

In the seventh the Tigers scored two more to go ahead 3–1, and in the eighth they put it out of reach. With Casey Cox now pitching for Washington, Cash hit a homer, Kaline singled and Horton tripled to right. By the time the inning was over they had scored five more runs and the game ended 8–3 in favor of the Tigers.

All of a sudden the Tigers were a happy ball club, and they went to bed that night eager to get another crack at Washington the next day. But this was a year when, for the Tigers, happiness was a luxury they enjoyed only rarely.

The next day, August 10, the bomb dropped.

It was midmorning and the Tigers were at the Shoreham Hotel in Washington. Willie Horton came down from his room and saw a group of players gathered in the lobby, talking in hushed tones. When he approached the huddle he learned at once what had happened.

Charlie Dressen was dead.

Willie Horton stood, staring into space, when he heard the news. He could not believe it. The peppery, spry little Dressen —dead? It made no sense whatever.

But it was true, and the knowledge seeped through the shock that numbed Horton.

"I can't believe it," he said slowly. "Not Charlie."

All the Tigers were shaken by the news.

"He was a fine manager," one of them said. "He got the best out of everyone."

"You wonder why a thing like this happens," said another.

Horton sat down in a chair. He felt as if his world was crumbling around him. The man who had helped him most in baseball was dead. The man who had had the most confidence in him was gone. For a moment the thought ran through his mind that he would never again be able to play baseball. Never again.

But life had to go on, and Jim Campbell had already indicated that, with Charlie gone and Swift unlikely to return, Frank Skaff would handle the club for the rest of the season.

The hospital said that Dressen's death was the result of a coronary arrest. The next day, with the Tigers on the road and unable to attend, a high requiem mass was held at which the Reverend Father James W. Bodary officiated. He summed up the Tigers' feelings for Dressen with these poignant words:

"Before God, I don't think Charlie Dressen had to slide home. I think he scored standing up."

A second memorial mass was set for a future date when the Tigers would be able to attend.

That night Willie Horton and the rest of the Tigers took the field with black armbands on their uniforms and sadness in their hearts. Nothing went well that night, nor for a number of nights after that. The Tigers were a team in distress, and they played as if they were in a trance. They had their moments, as all teams do, but they did not play up to their potential. By August 29, with only about a month to go, the Tigers were still in second place, but they were a whopping fourteen games out of first.

The season ground on without much change in the situation. The Tigers won their share of games, and Baltimore even began to lose some, but the wide gap between the two teams was too much to close. And once, when the Tigers beat the Cleveland Indians twice and Baltimore lost, Skaff said, "So the Orioles lost again, eh? Who knows? Things might get pretty interesting before this is over."

But that was whistling in the dark. The real battle, so far as the Tigers were concerned, was not for the pennant. It was second place that was at stake, with the Minnesota Twins the challengers.

The fight for second place raged through the month of September, with the Tigers holding a slight edge. Then, on September 26, the Tigers received more depressing news in a very depressing year. Bob Swift had fallen into a coma and had been placed on the hospital's critical list.

Meantime, the search for a new manager was taking all the concentration of the Tiger front office. It was conceded that Frank Skaff was handling the team well, but the Tiger front office felt it was important to get a big-name manager, someone prominent in baseball whose name would mean something to Tiger fans. Al Lopez, living in retirement in Florida, was mentioned again. Ralph Houk of the Yankees was considered, and so was the bombastic Leo Durocher. And the Tigers, confused and depressed, kept on battling for second place.

The matter was finally decided in the last three games of the season. The Tigers were up against the pesky Kansas City A's and the result was disaster. Kansas City beat the Tigers three straight and knocked them permanently into third place. The triple defeat enabled the Minnesota Twins to grab second place by one game.

It had not only been a horrible season for the Tigers, but one of the most disastrous ever experienced by a major league club. It had all begun with bright new hope. Charlie Dressen had won the affection and cooperation of the club, and with promising new players coming into the limelight, it looked as if the Tigers would at last be a real contender. Then Dressen had been stricken and finally died. Bob Swift, his replacement, was also removed from action by a serious illness.

No team in the history of baseball had ever lost two managers through illness in a single season, and serving under three men had been a difficult situation for the hapless Tigers. They finally finished the season with 88 wins and 74 losses, ten games behind the pennant-winning Baltimore Orioles.

Willie Horton, after a slow start, had managed to put together a creditable season. He posted a .262 batting average in 146 games, collected 27 home runs and batted in an even 100.

"It wasn't too bad, considering everything," he told his wife. "But next year I hope to do better."

The Tiger brass was eager to push the depressing season behind them, and on the day following the last game of the year, they named their new manager for 1967. He was Mayo Smith, fifty-one-year-old New York Yankee scout who had managed both the Philadelphia Phillies and the Cincinnati Reds in the National League. Smith was signed to a two-year contract.

Swept out of office by the signing were acting manager Frank Skaff and coaches Mike Roarke, Stubby Overmire and Pat Mullin. They were eventually replaced by Tony Cuccinello, Wally Moses, Hal Naragon and Johnny Sain.

Then, on October 17, the final blow of a tragic season fell. Bob Swift passed away.

Chapter 13

The winter of 1966–67 was one of the loneliest and most miserable of Willie Horton's career. With the baseball season over, he had little to do except think of his troubles. And one of his most disturbing troubles was the fact that Charlie Dressen was no longer an influence in his life.

Horton missed Dressen in the same way he had missed his parents. Dressen had been more than a manager to him. He had been a man to whom Willie could bring his troubles and frustrations, a man who would help him to solve the complexities of his life.

During the winter months, when the excitement of baseball battle was over, Charlie Dressen would often call Willie Horton on the phone all the way from California, for no other reason than to talk to him and see if he could help him in any difficulties he might be having. Dressen knew, with the wisdom that goes with age, that Willie was in the process of growing up and that the pains of his transition from boy to man often had him confused and in need of counsel. And the phone calls and the advice he imparted to Willie were the therapy that would make the growing pains less severe.

Now Dressen was gone and there were no more phone calls. And Willie missed them.

"Maybe it would help," he said to Patricia, "if I went back to Puerto Rico and played ball this winter. It would help get a lot of things off my mind."

"If you think it would help you," Patricia said, "then that's what you should do."

"It'll help me keep in shape too," said Horton. "Otherwise I might put on weight." He smiled at the memory of that other winter in Florida when Dressen had made him slim down. "Charlie didn't like me showing up overweight," he said.

So Willie Horton went to Puerto Rico again and played ball for Mayaguez. While he was there he signed a $30,000 contract with the Tigers, but the fat contract and the change of scenery didn't dispel his loneliness. Besides, Willie was beset with another trouble. Toward the end of the Puerto Rican season, he twisted his ankle, and finally it became so tender that he was unable to play. Discouraged, he came back to Detroit in late December. Back home, he went to the Downtown YMCA to work the soreness out, and by January 10 the sprain had healed.

With the ankle in apparently good shape again, Horton began to see a silver lining in his future. Then one day he looked out the window of his home and saw that a heavy snowstorm had coated the sidewalks with snow and ice.

"I better salt that front walk," he said, "before somebody falls and gets hurt."

He went out with a large bag of salt and began to spread it over the slippery sidewalk. He was almost finished when he reached into the bag for a handful of salt and a severe pain shot through the back of his left hand. The sharp pain subsided immediately, and Horton shrugged his shoulders and ignored it.

That night Willie woke up in a cold sweat. His hand was throbbing with pain. Switching on a lamp, Willie looked at the offending hand. To his amazement his hand and the lower part of his arm were swollen so badly that the arm had torn the sleeve of his pajamas!

"It's one thing after another this winter," he said to his wife. "This looks like I'm in real trouble."

It was back to the hospital for Willie, and when the doctors looked him over they came to an immediate decision.

"You have a case of blood poisoning," they told Horton.

Fortunately, the hand was quickly cured. It took three days to alleviate the condition, and by the time spring training rolled around, Willie Horton was in what appeared to be fairly good physical shape.

Before he left for Florida, Horton gave voice to something he had been thinking about for some time. "You know what I'd like to do this season?" he said. "I'd like to wear Charlie Dressen's number seven as a kind of memorial to him. I wonder if they'd let me do that?"

"I don't see why not," said Patricia. "You have very strong feelings for him."

Horton nodded. "Yeah. I think I'll find out if I could do that."

Willie Horton had not yet recovered from the depression he'd experienced following Dressen's death. He was confused and lonesome, and that lonesomeness was compounded when he went to Florida alone, leaving Patricia and the two children behind. The year before, the family had experienced difficulty finding a place to stay and had commuted every day from Plant City, twenty miles from the training camp in Lakeland. Willie thought it best that he face the housing problem alone.

"I can always stay in the motel with the team," he told a reporter, "but you can't house a family of four in a motel—you have to have a house. Last year we couldn't find a place in Lakeland. There were places where Negro players could live, but you wouldn't want to bring your family to any of them. Next year I'm bringing my family down, though, if I have to live in Tampa and drive to Lakeland every morning."

It was the old story—inadequate housing for Negroes in the white-oriented South.

"Don't get me wrong, though," Horton said. "I haven't really had any trouble in Lakeland. I eat downtown and I go anywhere I want. There just aren't any houses."

When training camp opened, Willie Horton had changed his mind about wearing Charlie Dressen's number seven. When he suited up he had his 1966 shirt on. He looked at his sleeve, where a black band had been placed the year before and had now been removed, and he sighed.

"I guess I just have to accept the fact that it's over and the man's gone," he told a writer. "I thought for a while that I wanted to wear Charlie's number as a sort of memorial to him. But now I don't think he'd want it that way. He gave me number twenty-three when I came up, so I think I'll keep wearing it. Besides, I guess it wouldn't be fair to the other man."

The "other man" was Mayo Smith, the new Tiger manager.

As the tempo of spring training stepped up, Willie Horton lost some of his inwardness and again began doing the thing he did best—clouting baseballs out of sight. He quickly accommodated himself to Mayo Smith, recognizing right away that Smith was a sound baseball man who knew what he was doing, and also knew what his players were doing wrong. Horton also had an immediate rapport with the new batting coach, Wally Moses, who had been a pretty fair American League hitter himself.

"You don't have to hit the ball hard to get a hit," Moses told Horton. "Don't get in the habit of overswinging. Timing is the most important thing in the world to a hitter."

To help Willie's and the rest of the team's hitting, Moses had a technique of standing next to the batting cage and telling hitters when to swing. When the ball came toward the plate, Moses would shout, "Hit!" and the batter would start his swing. Willie liked the technique. He'd stand in the cage, bat cocked, and start to swing as Moses said, "Hit!" More often than not Horton would drill the ball into the outfield, and on many occasions over the fence.

All spring long the sound rang out at the Tiger training camp. "Hit! Hit! Hit!"

The batters swung, the sweat poured from their bodies, the ball ricocheted off of outfield walls.

Meantime, Johnny Sain was working with the pitchers, especially the three youngsters, Denny McLain, Mickey Lolich and Joe Sparma. Sain had come to the Tigers from Minnesota, where he had fashioned a pitching staff that had led the Twins to a pennant in 1965. The Tiger brass was counting strongly on two factors to lead them to a pennant in 1967—the emergence of the "three young arms" of their pitching staff and the power of Willie Horton.

Horton was acutely aware of this expectation on the part of Tiger management, but it didn't disturb him. Ever since he had joined the club he had been pointing to a pennant and the World Series.

"Nothing else counts," he said on other occasions. "This team is going to go all the way one of these years."

Horton wasn't the only one who considered the Tigers strong pennant contenders. The press was giving the team a big preseason buildup. Some baseball writers actually picked them for first place, while others thought the Baltimore Orioles would win with the Tigers pushing them down the wire.

"They have a good hitting club," most of the writers said,

"and with Johnny Sain bringing the pitchers along—who knows? —they might be the surprise team of the league."

Unfortunately, this kind of preseason talk had been heard all too often by Detroit fans. For years the Tigers had looked good on paper, but just about the time the fans became steamed up over their prospects, the Tigers would slide out of the race. So Detroit followers were content to sit back and wait.

"They have to show me," said one fan. "I'm through getting excited about the pennant in this town and then being let down."

There was strong reason for the fans' doubt. The Tigers hadn't won the pennant since 1945, and in that year Willie Horton was only a bawling three-year-old baby in Arno, Virginia. Today, as the team's leading slugger, he could see a pennant in the offing.

"This is a good team," he said during spring training. "And you know what makes it good? Everybody looks like they love each other. I'm not kidding, everybody gets along fine."

He thought for a moment and then continued. "Last year and the year before we thought that maybe we had a chance to win the pennant. This year we're more positive. We have that feeling that we will win it."

"Willie," said a sportswriter, "last season you drove in a hundred runs, and you were the only player in the American League to accomplish this in both 1965 and 1966. How many RBIs do you think you can get this year?"

Horton's face split in a grin. "I never keep track of them," he said.

"You said the same thing last year," the writer told him.

"That's right, I did. And it's the truth. Tell you what—you do the counting and tell me how many when the season's over."

The writer went away shaking his head. "You don't get much out of that guy," he said to a fellow reporter.

"What he says is true, though," said his partner. "He *doesn't* count 'em."

With optimism riding high, it was the Tigers' misfortune to suffer another bad break before the season started. In the last week of the exhibition season, Willie Horton hit a ball to the infield and started for first base. Halfway there a pain shot through his left leg. He pulled up lame and hurting at first base.

Bill Behm, the Tiger trainer, rushed out to Horton at once. Willie was walking in circles, limping and trying to get the pain out of his leg.

"Man, I pulled something!" he exclaimed.

Horton was helped off the field and taken to the clubhouse. Stretched out on a rubbing table, Behm worked over him.

"It's a badly pulled muscle," Behm said. "It's hard to say how long he'll be out."

Discouraged by this latest blow to their fortunes, the Tigers headed north. On the way they played several games with Willie sitting on the bench nursing his painful left leg. He was disgusted and discouraged. He felt as though fate had dealt him a low blow. Here he was, primed for the season, hoping to help the team to their first pennant in twenty-two years, and now this injury threatened to keep him out of the opening game. It didn't seem fair.

The Tigers opened their season against the California Angels in Anaheim, and despite the absence of the injured Horton, the lineup they presented for the opener was an impressive one. The outfield consisted of Al Kaline in right, Jim Northrup in center and Gates Brown substituting for Horton in left. The infield had Don Wert at third, Dick Tracewski at short, Dick McAuliffe at second and Norm Cash at first. Behind the plate was Bill Freehan, and on the mound was Denny McLain.

And it was Mayo Smith's first chips-down game as Tiger manager.

Chapter 14

The 1967 season started auspiciously for the Detroit Tigers. George Brunet, the Angel pitcher who was something of a nemesis to the Tigers, beat them in the opening game, 4–2. But the Tigers bounced back quickly, and by the end of ten days they were in first place with six wins and three losses.

During this period Willie Horton sat forlornly on the bench, watching his teammates play. It was a frustrating experience for him. He loved baseball, and watching others play while he nursed a sore leg depressed him. But the pulled muscle was a painful and stubborn injury, and it was not responding to the treatment given it by trainer Bill Behm and team physician Dr. Russell Wright.

It was not until April 30 that Horton got into the box score as a pinch hitter, and then it was in a historic game that will be remembered long in the annals of baseball. The Tigers were playing Baltimore that day, and on the mound for the Orioles was Steve Barber. Never in his lifetime had Barber been in such incredibly good form. Fans in the stands sat in open-mouthed wonder—and his teammates did the same—as Barber mowed down the Tiger batters one after another. Halfway through the game the fans began to realize that Barber had a no-hitter going. They sat breathlessly through the sixth, seventh, eighth, and still no Tiger batter had even come close to getting a hit off him.

When the Tigers came to bat in the ninth inning, they were trailing the Orioles, 1–0, and the tension could be felt all over the park as Barber took the mound for the final inning.

The ninth inning turned out to be one of the most unforgettable innings in baseball history.

Norm Cash was the first man up, and as he strode toward the plate Willie Horton edged forward on his seat in the dugout. Horton had not yet played an inning of baseball for the Tigers since the start of the season, and he would have given his right arm—or better yet, his injured left leg—for a chance to appear in this historic contest.

Barber, a little awed perhaps at the prospect of a no-hitter, walked Cash. Immediately manager Mayo Smith sent in Dick Tracewski to run for Cash. After all, the score was only 1–0, and the Tigers were still in the ball game.

Ray Oyler, a light hitter, was next up, but Barber, having difficulty with his control, walked him too. Speedy Jake Wood then went in to run for Oyler.

Now there were two men on base with nobody out. It was a threatening situation, but still the Tigers had not had a hit.

Earl Wilson, a good-hitting pitcher, was given the bunt sign, and he laid down a perfect one along the third base line that moved the base runners to second and third.

Mayo Smith looked down the bench, trying to decide on a pinch hitter for Dick McAuliffe.

"Willie," he said, "can you hit?"

Horton jumped up from the bench so eagerly he almost hurt his leg again.

"Sure I can!"

He went out to the plate, feeling the ever-present pain as he walked. He was afraid his timing would be off because of his long absence from the game, but he could try. Mayo Smith was looking for the long ball that would put the game on ice, or at least a fly ball deep enough to score the tying run from third.

But neither happened. Willie swung at a curve and lifted a foul fly down the third base line—and trudged back to the dugout half in anger at himself.

That made it two outs with two men still on base. And still no hits for the Tigers.

Now it was Mickey Stanley's turn to bat. Barber, having regained his control, got one ball and two strikes on the young outfielder. That put him within one pitch of a no-hit game. All he needed was one more strike.

Barber went into his stretch, brought the ball to his chest for a momentary pause, then delivered. The ball went into the dirt and then skipped by catcher Larry Haney. Tracewski raced home from third with the tying run and Wood moved to third!

The Tigers had tied the score in the ninth inning, had a man on third again, with two out—and still Barber had not allowed a hit!

Barber was unsteadied by his misfortune. He walked Stanley, and Hank Bauer, manager of the Orioles, strode from the dugout to the mound.

It was a difficult decision to make—taking a pitcher out of the game when he had a no-hitter going—but Bauer did it. He felt that Barber's bad ninth inning was jeopardizing the game and he had to make the move.

Barber walked to the Orioles' dugout with his head down and with a no-hitter still hanging fire!

The first man to face reliefer Stu Miller was third baseman Don Wert. Wert bounced to Luis Aparicio at short who scooped up the ball and tossed it easily to second baseman Mark Belanger for a force-out of Stanley at second.

It would have been the third out of the inning, but Belanger dropped the throw. Jake Wood raced home with the Tigers' go-ahead run!

When Al Kaline grounded for the third out, the Tigers had a 2–1 lead in the ninth inning without having managed a hit! The game ended that way—one of the most astounding no-hit losses in baseball history!

And just to make it more dramatic, the win put the Tigers in sole possession of first place. Leading the league with ten wins and six losses, Detroit was trailed by New York, one-half game behind; Boston and Chicago, one game behind; and Baltimore, two games behind.

After his one stint as a pinch hitter, Willie Horton was back on the bench again. He suffered in idleness through several more games, worrying about whether or not he would ever get back in the lineup, whether or not this season was to be a total loss to him.

One day he remembered what his high school coach, Sam Bishop, had once told him when he was suffering an injury. "You can't quit because you're hurting," Bishop had said. "A good athlete plays over his injuries. Sometimes you have to bear pain if you want to be successful."

The words, uttered in 1959, came back to him now. He turned to his wife. "I've got to play," he decided. "I can't let an injury ruin my chances."

He went directly to the telephone and called Mayo Smith. When he had the manager on the phone he said, "I can't sit out any more of them. I want you to play me."

"You think you can do it, Willie?" Smith asked.

"I think I can. I want to try it anyway."

Mayo Smith admired Willie's determination and the next day,

May 5, Willie Horton was back at his accustomed place in left field. That day the Tigers beat Baltimore, 4–0, but Horton went 0-for-3. He had missed thirteen games and his timing was not sharp.

The next day he got his first hit of the season, a single, and the Tigers won again, 4–1.

The games were painful to Horton. Running caused the pain to shoot through his leg, but he set his jaw against the pain and forced himself to play.

On May 10 he had a real chance to test the injured leg. Detroit was playing Cleveland in spacious Municipal Stadium. The Indians took a 1–0 lead early in the game, and when the fourth inning opened Horton was the leadoff man for the Tigers.

Sonny Siebert was on the mound for Cleveland, and trying to pitch too carefully, he walked Horton. The next hitter sacrificed and Horton made second easily. It brought Norm Cash to the plate.

Horton took a modest lead off second and thought, *I wish he'd tag one. Then I'd have to leg it for home and I could really find out if this leg will hold up.*

Horton got his chance. Cash ripped a single into right field and Horton raced to third, rounded the bag, and went in to score the tying run.

To Horton's surprise, the leg caused him only a little pain. In fact, Willie was so delighted at the way it felt that he went to bat in the sixth inning and hit his first home run of the 1967 season, a 440-foot drive to deep center. The Tigers won the game, 4–2, and maintained a half-game lead over second place Chicago.

In the clubhouse Willie talked to reporters, all of them anxious to know about his injury.

"It feels all right once I get it warmed up," he said, "but the leg is plenty sore before that. I was hoping Cash would get a hit so I could try the leg out by running hard. And it felt pretty good."

"So then you decided to hit a home run so you could trot around the bases slowly?" asked a writer.

Horton grinned. "Sure. I don't know what kind of a pitch it was. It looked like a fast ball that ran away from me. I hit it straight away instead of pulling it."

Suddenly, now, the Tigers were burning up the league. They moved to Boston and whipped the Red Sox 10–8 in a slugfest. It was their seventh win in a row and their eleventh in the last thirteen games. They had to come from behind with six runs in the ninth to win—and that was symbolic of the kind of ball they were playing.

The next day, though, Boston won a doubleheader against the Tigers and shoved them into second place, one and a half games back of the Chicago White Sox.

Horton played both games and went 5-for-9.

"It looks," said Mayo Smith, "as though Willie's getting his timing back."

A few days later Horton enjoyed another good day when he led Detroit to an easy 8–1 win over Washington by hitting two home runs. In the clubhouse afterward he was the butt of jokes.

"So Willie's hurtin', eh? Everybody should hurt like him!"

"Don't worry! Horton knows what he's doing. He hits the ball out of the park so he won't have to run on that bad leg. He just trots around, like a broken-down mare."

Typically, Willie took the kidding in stride and placed a more serious emphasis on his problem.

"It's been kind of tough," he said. "When I started to play again I found out I couldn't swing naturally, because I had trouble striding and putting my weight on my left foot. Wally Moses has helped me a lot. He's making a better hitter out of me by getting me to use my wrists more. I think I'm becoming a more flexible hitter."

On May 21 the Tigers got the scare of their lives. Detroit was playing New York and Joe Pepitone of the Yankees drove a long fly to left center. Horton turned and raced toward the fence—and smashed headlong into the barrier. He went down like a felled ox and did not get up.

Mayo Smith leaped from the bench with the trainer and ran into left field to see if Willie was badly hurt. In the process, Smith pulled a muscle in his leg.

The stretcher bearers had raced to the scene too, but it turned out that Horton only had the wind knocked out of him. A writer described the incident this way:

"Willie Horton was unhurt, but Mayo Smith hobbled back to the dugout with a gimpy leg. Receiving Hospital reported that the wall will also recover."

Willie Horton continued to play. He had constant pain in his left leg, but he remained philosophical about it.

"Pain is nothing new to an athlete," he said one day. "Take Mickey Mantle. There is a man I really admire. I'd heard how they taped up Mickey but it wasn't until I made the All-Star team a few years ago that I saw what they had to do to get him ready for a game. He's remarkable. It hasn't been easy for him, and he's a great one. I can accept the same thing."

On Memorial Day the Tigers met the Chicago White Sox in a twin bill that was packed with drama. With the Tigers holding a perilous 2–1 lead in the fifth inning of the first game, a bizarre incident occurred. Al Kaline was the first man up in the inning and he cracked a double to left field. It was Horton's turn to bat. Gary Peters was on the hill for the Sox and he looked the big slugger over carefully. Some pitchers had the idea that quick-pitching Horton was a help, and almost before Willie was anchored in the batter's box Peters ripped a fast ball down the alley.

This time, though, it wasn't too quick. Willie swung and the ball shot into center field. Kaline tore around third and headed for the plate, and the White Sox center fielder fired the ball home. With the throw going to the plate, Horton rounded first and headed for second, the injured leg throbbing at every step.

Kaline was safe at the plate and the ball was thrown back to Ron Hansen at second in an attempt to cut down Willie. Horton hit the dirt and went into second sliding. The spikes on his shoe brushed Hansen's leg, and the Chicago second baseman turned red with anger.

"That was a deliberate spiking!" he snapped.

"I didn't do it on purpose," Horton denied.

"Not much, you didn't!"

Horton leaped to his feet. His own temper could be aroused easily, and he was ready to fight Hansen right on the spot for what he considered an unfair accusation. But manager Mayo Smith rushed from the dugout and began to push Horton away. In the melee around second Horton stepped on Mayo Smith's toe, and Smith went limping back to the dugout.

The Tigers won both games, 4–2 and 4–3, with Horton driving in the winning run in the first game and tying the second with his seventh homer of the year. One writer, in his account of the incident at second base, said:

"Mayo Smith pulled a leg muscle a week ago running out to check on Willie after he ran into a wall. This time he got his toe stepped on. Mayo will probably be put in the hospital by Horton before the season is out."

Horton laughed at the comment. "I didn't spike Hansen on purpose and I didn't step on Mayo's toe on purpose—and, man, I didn't run into that wall on purpose either!"

The double victory was important to the Tigers. It put them in first place again.

Chapter 15

The condition of Willie Horton's leg improved very little as the season ground on. In the morning he would get out of bed and experience difficulty even walking on it. Later, as he forced himself to use the leg, it would get more agile—but the pain never left it entirely.

Dr. Russell Wright tried many things—the whirlpool bath, massaging and occasional injections of cortisone—but the pain lingered.

"They say I'll have to have an operation on it," he told writers on several occasions, "but I'm not going to have it now. I could quit and have the operation any time, but I want to stay with the team. I can stand the pain if we win."

When the team was at home, Willie had another "doctor" working on his leg. It was his old high school coach, Sam Bishop. Bishop, who had retired as a coach at Northwestern High School, lived within a block of Horton, and he would come over in the morning and massage the big slugger's ailing leg for him. One time, when the pain was particularly excruciating, Bishop knocked on Horton's door.

"How's it feel today?" Bishop asked.

"Not very good. I can hardly walk on it."

"Sit down and let me massage it," Bishop said, and a minute later he was working on Horton's leg with supple fingers.

"You'll be able to play," he said.

"I hope so," said Horton, "but the way it feels now, I couldn't walk up to the plate."

Bishop smiled. "Like I always said, Willie, you have to play with pain sometimes. You have to live with it. You can't give up."

"I'm not going to give up, Sam," Horton said. "I'm not ever going to quit. I've always dreamed of playing with a major league team, and I'm not going to let a little pain stop me now."

That evening Horton was on hand for a Tiger night game and he played, just as he had promised himself he would.

"Sam Bishop," he said, "is a wonderful man. I really think he's keeping me in the game with the massaging he does."

Manager Mayo Smith was, naturally, concerned about Horton's injury, and often he would ask him if he wanted to play or not. The answer was always in the affirmative. But Mayo did rest Willie on several occasions, and for much of the early season Horton was in and out of the lineup.

Many ballplayers would have been willing to sit on the bench for the season had they been suffering half as much as Horton, but Willie was not one to dog it.

"I want to play as much as possible," he said. "I think this experience is making a man out of me."

Even though it was only the first of June, the race in the American League was already showing signs of being a dogfight to the wire. Four teams were bunched at the top—the Detroit Tigers, Chicago White Sox, Minnesota Twins and Boston Red Sox. The most tenacious competitor, as far as the Tigers were concerned, was Chicago. The White Sox were rarely more than one game behind the Tigers, hanging in there waiting for the Detroiters to falter.

On June 6 the Tigers drubbed the Athletics twice, 11–1 and 7–1, and one of the highlights of the game was a hit by Horton. It was not an ordinary hit. Kansas City's Municipal Stadium had a sign shaped like a baseball perched above the fence in home run territory. A local bank advertised that they would pay $3,500 to any player hitting the sign.

Horton drove the ball toward the sign and a lot of people said the ball hit the sign and dropped back onto the field, a $3,500 home run for Willie. But the umpires ruled that the ball hit the top of the fence and bounced back for a mere double. Horton didn't get the money or the home run, but he laughed off his misfortune.

"I miss the homer more than I miss the money," he said. "The guys on the team would have made me split up the cash with them anyway."

By June 10 the Tigers were still leading the White Sox by half a game—and then disaster struck. Detroit lost four games in a row and fell to second place, a game behind Chicago.

When the losing streak went to five in a row, Mayo Smith took cognizance of the situation with a statement to the writers.

"We're starting to press a little, but we'll snap out of it," he said. "This is a solid ball club."

The following day the Tigers were in Minnesota to meet the Twins, another team that was breathing on their necks. Dean Chance, Minnesota's hottest pitcher, started for the Twins. He was in excellent form. By the end of the fifth inning the Twins had a 5–1 lead, and it looked as if Chance would breeze to an easy victory. Then came one of those dramatic innings that occur only once or twice in a season.

Al Kaline led off for the Tigers with a single. Willie Horton then rapped a single to left, sending Kaline to third, and when the Twins' left fielder Bob Allison bobbled the ball Kaline scored. Norman Cash walked and Freehan singled, scoring Horton. Cash, though, was out trying to go to third on the hit. Mickey Stanley beat out an infield hit, and Gates Brown came off the bench to bat for the light-hitting Ray Oyler.

Dean Chance was removed from the game and Jim Ollom came in to try to get the Tigers out. But he walked Brown to load the bases, and then Jim Price ripped another single to left to score two runners. Dick McAuliffe walked to load the bases again, and Mudcat Grant came in to pitch for Minnesota. Don Wert hit a single, scoring two more runners. That brought up Kaline for the second time in the inning and he singled again. Horton, up for his second time, also singled. A wild pitch and a passed ball got Kaline and Horton around the bases.

When the inning ended the Tigers had racked up ten runs, nine of them earned, and all eight hits in the inning were singles. Detroit won the game 15–10.

But this spectacular victory was a rare one. The Tigers were simply not playing up to their capacity, and by June 25 they were in dire straits. They had lost thirteen out of their last eighteen games, mostly because the pitching staff had failed them. Starters had been unable to go the route and the relievers were arm-weary. The pitching staff had given up seventy-five home runs, tops in the American League, and the result was that the Tigers were now in second place, four full games behind the Chicago White Sox—and only six and a half games out of *last place!*

On June 27 the Tigers suffered two more cruel blows to their chances. Al Kaline, their star outfielder, slammed his bat in the rack in a fit of anger at his own performance and smashed his right hand in the process. The broken hand put Kaline on the disabled list for twenty-one days. About the same time Gates

Brown, their most effective pinch hitter, was sidelined with a hand injury.

To replace these two players, the Tigers called up Lenny Green from their Toledo farm club and purchased Jim Landis from the Houston Astros in the National League.

The absence of Kaline placed an added burden on Willie Horton, who had to do most of the hitting for the team. Struggling to make up for Kaline's departure, he struck out twice and hit into a double play the very next day. But he also hit a single to break a 3–3 tie, and Mayo Smith said happily, "I'm not worried about him."

The fans were worried, though. And the oddsmakers were saying that without Kaline the Tigers were out of the race. But, amazingly, Detroit won six games in a row with Kaline out of the lineup, and continued to be a factor in the pennant race.

Early in July, Horton's leg became so sore that Mayo Smith finally put him on the bench.

"Rest a few days," he said. "Maybe it'll feel better."

With three key men on the bench, the All-Star Game came along to give the hurting Tigers a few days' respite. But when the season resumed, the Tigers looked drab and lifeless. Horton was still out of the game, Wert was back in but hobbling, Kaline was sidelined and the pitching staff was struggling. In mid-July Horton finally got back in the lineup and found his timing had been affected by the layoff. He went 0-for-3 against Washington and the Tigers lost, 3–2.

But the 1967 pennant race was an unbelievable one. Despite the Tigers' poor play, they were still only three and a half games behind the leading White Sox, even though they had lost fourteen out of thirty-seven games.

On July 17, though, they slid into fourth place on a loss to Boston, and they were then four and a half games off the pace.

Horton tried his best to keep the Detroit team afloat. But there was no doubt that his injured leg restricted his play. It slowed him up in the field, and made base-running a torturous effort. In one game Horton got credit for one of the longest singles on record—simply because he couldn't run. The ball traveled 400 feet against the center field wall, but Horton, limping badly, couldn't get beyond first base. Mayo Smith put in a pinch runner and took Willie out of the game.

"I guess it's best for the team," Horton admitted. "Maybe I'm hurting their chances by being in there. But it sure bothers me to sit on that bench."

Five days later Horton returned to the lineup. The Tigers were playing the New York Yankees at Detroit that night, and Mayo Smith was making out his lineup during the Tigers' batting practice. Horton's name wasn't on the scorecard. Smith looked at the batting cage and noticed Horton was up there taking his cuts. In succession, he hit two pitches into the left field stands. Smith started to erase a name from the lineup card.

"Maybe I better put him in," he decided.

Horton responded well. The Yanks jumped away to a 2–0 lead early in the game, and when the third opened Dick McAuliffe was the first hitter up. McAuliffe thumped a single to right. Don Wert then drilled a single through the box, and Norm Cash hit a third single to right. The score was now New York 2, Detroit 1 —and Horton was up.

Horton didn't wait. He blasted a home run into left field to put the Tigers ahead. They finally won 11–4. Horton had himself an evening with four out of five.

On July 23 tragedy struck Detroit. Riots rocked the city, and officials imposed a curfew. The Tigers were scheduled to play the Baltimore Orioles at Tiger Stadium that night, but instead the game was rescheduled for the Baltimore ball park. The Tigers went to Baltimore, played an inning and a half, and were rained out. It was one of baseball's oddities: The only game in history that was canceled twice in two different cities on the same day!

On July 28 Al Kaline returned to the lineup after missing twenty-five games, during which the Tigers won fourteen and lost eleven. The standings at the end of July had Chicago still clinging to first place with Boston two games out, Detroit four games back, and Minnesota trailing by five.

Tiger fans, growing weary with the teams' inability to improve in the standings, began to complain that the Tigers were too serene about losing. Newspaper dispatches said that there seemed to be no response in the Tiger clubhouse after losing a game. Mayo Smith, irritated by the reports, put the record straight.

"Sure, I know the team has played some bad baseball lately. But no one should call them ho-hum contenders. They're hollering and pulling for each other as much as could be asked of any ball club."

Horton was one who was doing a lot of hollering—from the bench. He even pulled for Lenny Green, who was substituting for him in left field as the big slugger sat on the bench and nursed an aching leg. Horton got back in the lineup for a game with Baltimore, hit a double and aggravated the injury again running out the hit.

By mid-August the American League race had become one of the hottest of all time. On August 14 the Minnesota Twins held first place, Chicago was second one game behind, Detroit was one and a half games back in third, the California Angels were fourth and only two and a half games out, and Boston trailed by three.

In the last half of August the Tigers met the Twins in a five-game showdown series and won three of them. This knocked the Twins out of the lead and put Chicago and Boston in a tie for first place, with the Tigers only a half-game back.

It was that kind of a race.

And during this crucial time Willie Horton was unable to play. He fretted and fidgeted, paced the dugout, sat down, got up again.

"Man, it's worse sitting here than playing," he said.

As the race wore on, the four teams at the top—Detroit, Minnesota, Boston and Chicago—kept trading positions. On August 26 the Boston Red Sox were first. The next day it was the Twins. By the end of August it was Boston again, with the Twins and Tigers only a half game back.

Horton got back in the lineup on August 30, determined to play with pain through the critical month of September. But on September 1 the Tigers showed signs of jitters in a game against Minnesota. The pressure, it seemed, was beginning to tell on the team.

Eddie Mathews, the thirty-three-year-old infielder obtained on waivers from the Houston Astros as pennant insurance, made two throwing errors that gave Minnesota two runs. Then, in the third inning, Horton contributed a faux pas to the affair. The Twins' Bob Allison was on third and Rich Rollins was at bat. Rollins tagged a pitch hard and drove it on a line to Willie in left field.

Horton caught the ball, thinking it was the third out, and lackadaisically trotted in several steps before he realized that Allison was scoring after the catch. The Tigers lost the game as the result of the errors of commission and omission and dropped into third place, two games behind the league-leading Boston Red Sox.

"I don't know what I was thinking," Horton muttered afterward. "I could have thrown Allison out. He's got a bad leg like mine. I guess we all messed this game up."

As the teams rolled into September, the race became incredible.

The four leading teams were in a virtual tie, the standings looking like this:

	W	L	Pct.
Minnesota	78	61	.561
Chicago	78	61	.561
Boston	79	62	.560
Detroit	79	62	.560

Two days later the Tigers had jumped from fourth to a tie for first place by beating Chicago. Detroit and Minnesota were now deadlocked with 80 wins and 62 losses each, Boston was a half game behind and Chicago one game out.

On September 9 the Tigers opened a critical three-game series with the White Sox at Chicago. Gary Peters was pitching for the Sox and he was in rare form. At the end of eight innings the Tigers were behind, 3–0, and Peters was pitching magnificently.

Willie Horton faced Peters in the ninth and lifted a long fly to left field. There was a brisk wind blowing in from left and it held up the ball enough to allow the left fielder to catch it against the wall. Disappointed, Horton trudged back to the dugout. And then it started.

Chicago's Ken Berry started to ridicule Horton from the White Sox dugout. He waved a towel—a crying towel—and Horton began to burn slowly. When he reached the Tiger dugout he made a thumbs-down gesture to Berry.

The ridicule of their top slugger evidently supplied a spark to the Tigers that had been lacking all through the game. They rallied for three runs, then four, then five—finally seven. When Horton came up for the second time in the same inning, Berry said nothing. Horton drilled a two-run single to center. The Tigers won the game, 7–3.

In the happy Tiger clubhouse, Willie Horton was beaming with satisfaction.

"They asked for it," he said gloatingly, "and we gave it to them."

"What about this guy Berry?" asked a writer.

"Oh, him—he's flaky. He's always on somebody." Horton shrugged his huge shoulders. "Just because my hit didn't go in the stands, he got on me. But I think we silenced him in that ninth inning. He didn't say a word the next time I went up. I think we shook up their whole team."

"It might be the turning point for Chicago," Jerry Lumpe added.

A photographer was taking pictures of some of the top hitters in the game, among them Norm Cash and Jim Northrup. Cash waved Willie over.

"C'm on!" he yelled. "Get over here. We have to integrate this picture."

Willie limped over on his bad leg and grinned for the photographer. A writer, noticing, asked, "How's that foot?"

"Not bad," he said. "When we win the World Series I'm going to soak it in champagne!"

But the Tigers dropped two games to Chicago after their dramatic victory, and by the middle of September the three contenders were still virtually tied for first place.

Detroit played Washington at Tiger Stadium on September 15 in what turned out to be another dramatic game. Washington had a 4–1 lead going into the last of the eighth, but catcher Bill Freehan hit a home run with two on in the Tiger half to tie the score. Washington failed to score in the top of the ninth, and it was up to the Tigers to pull the game out in their half.

Casey Cox was pitching for the Senators, and he got Ed Mathews on a pop-up. Dick McAuliffe then singled, and Fred Lasher, the Tiger relief pitcher, moved him to second with a sacrifice bunt.

That brought up Al Kaline and the Washington strategy was

to walk him and pitch to Horton. There was a reason for this move. Horton had had a bad day, striking out three times, and the impatient Detroit crowd was beginning to boo him.

On the first pitch from Cox, Horton lifted a foul fly behind the plate that looked like curtains. But catcher Paul Casanova, staggering under it, missed it—and Horton had another chance.

Willie watched two balls go by, and then he swung at the next pitch. The ball went on a line into left field to bring in the winning run for the Tigers.

In the clubhouse a reporter said to Horton, "Nice going, big man."

"I'm the little man," said Horton and nodded toward Bill Freehan who had tied the score for the Tigers with his three-run homer in the eighth. "There's the big man."

The victory put the Tigers in a three-way tie with Boston and Minnesota. Each team had 84 wins and 64 losses. Chicago was now one and a half games behind.

Detroit fans were belatedly becoming excited about the prospects of a pennant. There seemed to be two trains of thought. One group said, "We've waited twenty-two years for a pennant winner and maybe this is finally the year." The other group said, "Don't get excited. The Tigers will blow it as usual."

Actually, none of the four clubs seemed capable of pulling away from the others. For the rest of the season they won a couple, lost a couple and stayed close together. As one wag put it, "I don't see how anybody can win it. We've got four mediocre teams trying to give it away."

Nevertheless, the torrid race went right down to the wire. Because of rainouts, the Tigers were forced to play two doubleheaders on the last two days of the season against the Los Angeles Angels. It was too much for them, especially for their overworked pitching staff. The best they could do was split. And, meantime, Boston beat Minnesota at Fenway Park to grab the

American League pennant on the last day of the season. The Tigers and the Minnesota Twins ended the season tied for second place—only one game behind!

It had been one of the most harrowing American League races in baseball history!

Chapter 16

The most important problem facing Willie Horton at the end of the 1967 season was his leg. Shortly after the season ended, Horton went to Henry Ford Hospital in Detroit, where a six-hour operation was performed. Surgeons removed two bone spurs and a growth the size of a golf ball from the area of his Achilles tendon. And while he lay on his back in the hospital, staring up at the clinical-white ceiling, Willie Horton had plenty of time to think about his own future and that of the Tigers.

As to his own future, everything depended on the leg. He had missed forty games in 1967 and had appeared only briefly in many more. Statistically, it had been a lost season for him. He had batted only .274, hit 19 home runs and driven in a mere 67. For Horton it was a bad performance; he knew he could do better.

As for the Tigers, they had battled down to the final game for the pennant and had lost it, and this was a bitter disappointment to swallow. But Horton knew that the Tigers had a comparatively young team, balanced off by a few strong veterans, and there was certainly grounds for expecting that the Tigers would be in the running again in 1968. And maybe, this time, they could go all the way.

When Willie was released from the hospital and was again able to get around, he put baseball out of his mind for a while and renewed his dedication to the underprivileged youth of the city. He was active in a Detroit program designed to get high school dropouts back at their desks. He tried to get high school graduates jobs before they went back to the streets looking for trouble. At Northwestern High School, he used his reputation as a star athlete to organize the Northwestern Men's Club. This was a group of some thirty ex-athletes of the school who were interested in helping young boys. The group worked with the school to encourage boys to go into athletics, and they acted as chaperones at school dances and sporting events.

Often Willie would go into the ghetto alone, visiting rickety apartment houses and cheap saloons—the dismal scenes of his boyhood—looking for boys in trouble or about to get into trouble. And when he talked to them, and urged them to mend their ways, they listened—because he was Willie Horton, the Tiger star.

His message to youngsters, delivered simply and directly, gave them something to think about. "Don't get the idea that the world owes you a living," he would tell them. "The world doesn't owe anybody a living. You've got to earn what you get—and that's the way it should be, too. Don't ever forget that."

All of this came easily to Willie, who not only knew the problems these boys faced from personal experience, but who had been helped by such men as Sam Bishop, Damon Keith and Louis D'Annunzio.

"I had some people take an interest in me when I was young," he said, "and this is the least I can do for youngsters now. The future of our state, our country, the world is in the hands of the kids."

For all his winter work with boys, baseball was never completely out of his mind. He was eager to start the new season, a season he was sure would find the Tigers in the World Series. He reported early to the Tiger training camp at Lakeland to get started. Naturally, on his arrival, the big question asked by everyone concerned the operation he had gone through and the efficiency of his leg.

"It's still sore," he told a battery of reporters, "but the doctor said it would be. Anyway, I can stand a little pain. I'm going to start early with some running and hope to work out some of the soreness."

"You think it's going to be all right then?"

"I don't really know," Horton said honestly. "Maybe the soreness will never leave entirely. I'm prepared for that, too, and a little thing like pain isn't going to keep me back." His face split into a grin. "You know, I'm used to pain. My coach at Northwestern High kept telling me I had to play over pain if I wanted to be a successful athlete, and that's what I'll have to do."

Willie reached into his locker and pulled out a pair of special shoes. "See how they're built up inside?" he said. "That's to protect my heels. The doctors think it will help me. It's almost like a cast that fits around my heels for support. Like I say, I expect some pain and I'll just have to live with it. Like Mickey Mantle."

During spring training, 1968, Mayo Smith and the rest of the Tiger brass were vitally concerned with the improvement of Willie Horton's leg. They knew that the Tigers' chance to win the pennant depended in great degree on whether Willie Horton had a good year or a bad one. Had Willie been able to play in the forty games he missed the year before, it could very well have made the difference between winning the pennant and losing it by one game. This year it would be the same.

Fortunately, Horton's leg continued to improve as spring training progressed, and the faces of Tiger management began to brighten. Then, during the Grapefruit League games, Willie threw a scare into everyone from owner John Fetzer to the bat boy—including himself—on at least two occasions. Once he hurt his right shoulder diving for a ball and was sidelined a week. In another game he pulled a muscle behind his left knee running out a double. But overall, Horton had a fine spring training, batting a classy .340, hitting three circuit clouts and batting in nine runs.

As the team moved north a reporter said to Horton, "You're doing pretty well. Have you any goals for this season?"

Willie just smiled. In 1965 he had hit 29 home runs and collected 104 RBIs, and he knew he wanted to better that if he could. But he was too smart to go out on the limb.

"Some players set goals," he said carefully, "but I just like to go out there every day and do the best I can. What I really want out of baseball right now is an American League pennant for the people of Michigan."

The Tigers opened the season against the Boston Red Sox in Detroit, and they presented virtually the same lineup that had fallen one game short of the flag in 1967. Mickey Stanley had moved to first base to replace a slumping Norm Cash, and the rest of the infield consisted of Dick McAuliffe at second base, Ray Oyler at shortstop, and Don Wert at third. The outfield had Al Kaline in right, Jim Northrup in center, and Willie Horton in left. Bill Freehan was behind the plate and, in the opener, Earl Wilson was on the mound.

In the dugout, Mayo Smith's mind was half-tuned toward the progress of the opening game and half toward the progress of Willie Horton. Ballplayers do not always extend themselves in exhibition games, but now the chips were down and Mayo Smith watched Horton closely to see whether or not his leg would hold up under regular play. He was delighted to see Willie make several good running catches and go full-tilt in beating out a double to left field during the game. And although Detroit lost its opener, Willie's condition cheered the team.

"Maybe that boy is going to be okay," Smith said after the contest.

Shrugging off their opening day loss, the Tigers went on to post an impressive winning streak. And Willie Horton stayed in step by getting away to a fast personal start.

The Tigers won their second game of the new season, 5–2, and in this one Horton drove in one run with a long sacrifice fly and hit a double to start a two-run rally that put the game away. The next day the Tigers beat Chicago, 5–4, with Horton getting 2-for-4. Then Detroit hammered Boston, 9–2, and Willie collected three hits in six appearances.

"He's hitting and that's fine," said a teammate, "but best of all, he's running. That heel doesn't seem to slow him down."

It was true. While there was still slight pain, Willie was getting along very well indeed, and now he was looking for a big 1968 season.

With three straight wins under their belts, the Tigers met the Cleveland Indians in their home opener on April 17. It was a tough fight all the way, and at the end of nine innings the two clubs were tied, 2–2.

In the top of the tenth the Indians scored a run to make the score 3–2 in their favor, and the Tigers came up for their last chance to correct the situation. It looked like curtains for Detroit hopes when Mickey Stanley and Dick McAuliffe were both disposed of easily. Cleveland relief pitcher Eddie Fischer had only one more man to get to put the game away.

That man was the always-dangerous Kaline, and Fischer attempted to hit the corners on the Tiger batter. He missed and

Kaline walked. That brought up Willie Horton to cope with the fluttery knuckleball for which Fischer was famous.

It had not been a good game for Horton. He had failed to hit all day. Fischer's knuckler was an almost impossible pitch to hit, and Willie could think of a dozen pitchers he would rather face with the tying run on first base. It was a foregone conclusion that Fischer would feed nothing but the butterfly pitches to Horton this time.

He did. Two pitches went hop-skipping over the plate, but the third one didn't get by. It was a knuckler that broke down and away, and Willie caught it on the fat of the bat. He golfed the ball in a majestic arc and it fell into the left field seats for a game-winning home run.

Horton was a picture of happiness after the game. "No kidding," he said, "I was trying to go to right field. Wally Moses teaches us to go to right field on the knuckleball. I wasn't trying to pull it, and I didn't realize it was a homer until I rounded first base and looked at the third base coach. He was waving me around."

The dramatic victory was the opening gun in a season that would be marked with come-from-behind wins by the Detroit Tigers. Before the season ended the Tigers were to become known as the Sock-It-To-'Em Team, a nickname based on the fact that they were most dangerous from the seventh inning on.

The following day Detroit whipped Cleveland, 5–0, for their sixth straight win and found themselves in a tie with the Minnesota Twins for first place. Each team had a 6–1 record. Horton contributed a 450-foot homer, his second in two days, to pin down the victory.

On April 20 the Tigers beat Chicago, 4–1, for their seventh straight win, and when Minnesota lost, it put the Tigers in first place alone. The next day they played their first doubleheader and won both games, 4–1 and 4–2. That gave them nine wins in a row, and Detroiters began wondering if the Tigers were really as good as they looked.

All victory streaks must end, and the Tigers' came to a crashing halt in Cleveland. The Tigers lost the game, 2–0, but it was what happened in the seventh inning that sent a cold chill through Mayo Smith and his stalwarts.

Cleveland pitcher Steve Hargan hit a short fly to left field and Willie Horton came racing in. At the same time shortstop Ray Oyler faded back. The two players collided and Horton fell flat to the ground. When he did not get up, Mayo Smith and half the bench warmers rushed to his aid.

Horton was out cold. A few minutes later, as a hushed crowd looked on, Willie was carried from the field on a stretcher. In the clubhouse Dr. Eduardo Coligado made a preliminary examination.

"He hit his head pretty hard, but there appears to be no fracture," he announced. "To be safe, though, he'd better go into the hospital for observation."

Ray Oyler stood there shaking his head. "I was stunned for a moment," he said. "I think I hit him with either my shoulder or the back of my head."

Horton was found to be suffering from a concussion, and he did not return to the lineup until May 1. During his absence, though, the Tigers managed to cling to first place. They were a mere half game ahead of Minnesota, and they were scheduled to meet the Twins in a two-game series that was already being billed as "critical."

The Tigers' difficulty in the early season games had been hitting. Horton, although missing some games, was lambasting the ball at a .308 clip, but his mates were only hitting for a club average of .235. Pitching was holding the team together.

And pitching saved them again in the Minnesota series. The Tigers won the first game, 3–2, and lost the second in ten innings by the same score. The "critical" series left the two clubs in the same position as before.

The hitting slump continued as the Tigers met the Los Angeles Angels. Willie Horton hit two home runs in the first game of the series but received little help from the rest of the Detroit hitters. The Tigers lost, 6–5. The next day Horton hit another home run—his sixth of the year—but the rest of the Tigers failed to come through and they lost again, 7–2. The two losses permitted the Baltimore Orioles to climb into first place by a game and a half over Detroit. The Tigers salvaged the last game from Los Angeles when pitcher Denny McLain won his fourth straight victory by a 5–2 count.

Then came another important series, this time with Baltimore. It was a three-game set-to and it gave the Tigers a chance to make up their one-and-a-half-game deficit. But when the toothless Tigers were held to only one hit in the first game and beaten 4–0, moans went up all over Detroit. The Tigers were now two and a half games back.

But the next day the Tigers pulled out a squeaker, 2–1, and they were back within one and a half games of first place with the rubber game of the series coming up.

In the deciding game of the series Horton came through in splendid fashion. He singled to start the second inning, went to third on Don Wert's double and scored on Dick Tracewski's long fly. In the sixth he drove Kaline in from second with a single. Thus, Horton figured in two of the three runs the Tigers scored in a 3–1 victory over Baltimore. The Tigers were now just one-half game behind the league-leading Orioles.

The Tigers moved to Washington and slaughtered the hapless Senators 12–1—a refreshing display of hitting power for a change. Curiously, everyone hit in this one except Willie. He went 0-for-5. But the victory, coupled with a Baltimore loss, put the Tigers on top of the league by half a game. And in the next couple of days Detroit increased its first place lead to two full games.

Then, on May 14, Baltimore showed up at Tiger Stadium seeking revenge. The team ran into a rampaging Horton. In the second inning, with the score deadlocked, 0–0, Horton clobbered one of Dave McNulty's pitches into the left field seats for a solo homer. In the sixth, with the Tigers clinging to a perilous 2–0 lead, Kaline walked and Horton hit his second homer of the game to stretch the score to Detroit 4, Baltimore 0.

Earl Wilson was the winning pitcher by that score, and in the clubhouse he came over and shook hands with Horton. "Thanks, buddy," he said. "That homer in the sixth took the pressure off."

On May 16 the Tigers had an open date, so they went down to Toledo, Ohio, to play their Triple A farm club, the Mudhens. In the eighth inning, with the Tigers comfortably leading, manager Mayo Smith glanced down the dugout toward Horton.

"Manage the team, Willie," he said.

Horton came to with a jerk. "What?"

"You've been saying you'd like to handle the team. Go ahead."

Willie grinned broadly. Happily he began flashing signs to his men on the field—with some of the "take" signs irking the batters who were up there wanting to hit. It was a slightly hilarious two innings, with much kidding going on, and after the game Willie laughed and said:

"Man, that managing! It's easy!"

It was ten days later that the Tigers met Oakland on the west coast in what proved to be a disastrous game. The score was Oakland 7, Detroit 6, but that was not the important thing. It's what happened to individual Tigers that had the team reeling.

Al Kaline was struck by a pitch by Lew Krause and suffered a hairline fracture of his right forearm. The prognosis was that he would be lost to the team for at least three weeks.

Dick McAuliffe, after striking out, tossed his bat in disgust, then tripped over it and bruised his leg.

Willie Horton laid down a rare bunt and beat it out for a hit, but pulled a leg muscle in the process.

Late in the game Jim Northrup was hit in the back of the batting helmet with a pitch by Jack Aker. Northrup raced out to the mound and flattened Aker with one punch, and the two teams streamed out on the field for a free-for-all. Horton, nursing his bruised leg muscle, limped out on the field in his stocking feet determined to lay somebody low, but the scuffle ended before he got into action.

The next day Kaline was placed on the twenty-one-day disabled list which permitted the Tigers to recall a young outfielder named Wayne Comer from Toledo in the International League. The Tigers welcomed Comer, but he was obviously no Kaline and the injury to their star right fielder, everyone knew, would hurt their pennant chances. With Kaline out, Horton felt more than ever that he had to keep playing, to try to take up some of the slack. Despite the pain from his pulled leg muscle, Horton stayed in the game.

On the day following Kaline's injury, the Tigers met the Angels at Anaheim. In the first inning, after Mickey Stanley was out, Dick Tracewski singled, Northrup singled and Bill Freehan doubled home both runners. Willie then limped up to the plate and blasted a pitch into the stands—his twelfth homer of the season—so he could trot leisurely around the bases. The four runs held up and the Tigers won, 4–1.

The next day, with the Tigers leading by 1–0 in the sixth, Freehan walked and Horton drove his thirteenth homer 400 feet over the left center field fence to put the game on ice for Detroit, 3–0. When the Tigers also beat California the following day, 7–3, the Angels' manager, Bill Rigney, said, "The Tigers, this series, looked like the best team in the American League."

And Mayo Smith coyly replied, "Yes—our club does have a lot of potential."

On May 31 Detroit met the New York Yankees at Tiger Stadium. Mel Stottlemyre was on the mound for the Yanks, and Mickey Lolich pitched for the Tigers. It turned out to be a tight pitchers' duel, with the score still tied, 0–0, when the Tigers came to bat in the seventh inning.

Willie Horton was the first man to face Stottlemyre. He had not fared well against the Yankee pitcher, having failed to hit in three tries. But this time he smashed a home run into the left field stands and won the game for the Tigers, 1–0.

It was his fourteenth round-tripper and thirtieth RBI and the third time in the last eleven games that he had provided the game-winning blast.

"He's reading the pitchers now," said Mayo Smith. "But his leg is bothering him and he's not yet 100 percent."

The Tigers, despite the absence of Kaline, were still leading the league as the first of June dawned. They had won 28 games and lost 16, and they were two and a half games ahead of pursuing Baltimore.

On June 1 the Tigers met the Yanks again, and at the end of the sixth they were trailing the Bronx Bombers, 4–2. In the seventh Horton came up and drilled his fifteenth homer of the season—and his fourth in five games—into the left field seats. Norm Cash then hit another and the score was 4–4. The Tigers went on to win it, 5–4, in the late innings. That day, in addition to the homer, Horton had a single and a double and extended his hitting streak to fourteen straight games.

Then, unaccountably, Horton stumbled into a hitless slump. But still the Tigers continued to win. What was more important, they were showing an increased ability to come from behind in the late innings to win—the mark of a good ball club. By June 11 they had won thirteen games in their last trip to the plate. Even more important, they had now extended their first place lead over Baltimore to five games!

By now it was becoming apparent to all baseball observers that 1968 was the Year of the Pitcher. There were more low-score games being played than had been evident in the last decade. The pitchers seemed to have the upper hand in most games, batting averages were shrinking and teams were struggling to 1–0, 2–1 and 3–2 victories consistently.

On June 18 the Tigers had just such a game with the Boston Red Sox. The Tigers nursed a shaky 1–0 lead as they went into the sixth inning. In that inning Northrup singled, Freehan singled and Horton drilled one into center for a single that scored another run. It proved to be the winning run as the Tigers won 2–1.

A few days later, in New York, the Tiger bats sang a merrier tune—and just at the right time too. Detroit was behind, 5–1, as they came to bat against Steve Barber in the top of the seventh. They looked like sure losers, but the Yankees learned not to sell the Tigers short. Wayne Comer, substituting for the ailing Kaline, led off the inning with a walk. Barber promptly went out of the game and Steve Hamilton came in. Dick McAuliffe also walked and then Dick Tracewski doubled to left to drive in Comer.

The score was now 5–2.

That was enough for Hamilton. Out he went and in came Bill Monbouquette. Mickey Stanley poked a single to center, scoring two more runs.

Score now: Yanks 5, Detroit 4.

When Freehan singled, Fred Talbot came in from the bullpen to try to quell the riot. Willie Horton stepped to the plate, wondering if he could keep the rally going against this new pitcher.

Horton stood placidly and watched a pitch go by for a ball. Than Talbot cut the plate for a strike. The next one was a fast ball and Willie connected. The ball rode into left center and bounced against the distant barrier, and Horton legged it to third with a triple. Stanley and Freehan scored the tying and go-ahead runs on the hit.

Score: Detroit 6, New York 5!

Horton came in moments later on a sacrifice fly by Northrup. It was a big six-run inning and the Tigers eventually won the game 8–5. Again they had come from behind in the late innings.

The remarkable play of the Detroit team had widened the gap in the American League standings. The Tigers were now in first place, Cleveland trailed in second place by seven and a half games, Baltimore was now eight and a half games behind and Chicago was nine. And with the month of July just starting, some baseball experts were already conceding the pennant to the Tigers.

Chapter 17

Pennant fever was beginning to grip Detroiters as the Tigers began their July games. On July 2 they met the California Angels in Detroit and jumped on Tom Murphy in the first inning. With two out, Northrup doubled, Cash walked and a wild pitch to Willie Horton moved the runners to second and third. Horton promptly drilled a single to left that scored both runners. The Tigers won the game, 3–1, with Horton having driven in two of the three scores.

Since Cleveland lost, that increased the Tiger lead to eight and a half games, and reporters began to ask Mayo Smith about the Tigers' chances of winning the flag.

"The season is far from over," he hedged.

But on July 3 pitcher Denny McLain won his fifteenth game against only two losses, and talk got around that he was headed for a thirty-game season. On the fourth of July the Tigers created their own fireworks by blasting six home runs (Horton had one of them) to knock over California in a slugfest, 13–10.

By July 7 the Tigers had stretched their lead to nine and a half games, and Mayo Smith began getting telephone calls from people who hadn't called him in years. "Some I haven't heard from in twenty years," he said. "Nobody's asking for World Series tickets yet, but I think they're leading up to it." Then he grinned. "What I like about this club, it's not showing signs of tension or pressure, and I just hope we keep winning in the last half of the season as we did in the first half."

The All-Star Game interrupted procedures for a few days and then the Tigers resumed their run for the pennant. There was every reason for them to believe they could hold—and maybe stretch—their lead over the rest of the league. But baseball is a strange game and suddenly, for no reason they could fathom, they found themselves in a slump. They lost nine of the thirteen games following the All-Star contest, and the experts began to wonder if the Tigers were going to blow their chances again. In one of the losses Willie Horton strained some abdominal muscles trying to make a shoestring catch and that incident added to the Tigers' despair. But Horton ignored the new injury and was back in the lineup the next day.

"I have to keep playing," he said. "Hurt or no hurt, I have to stay in the lineup."

The losing streak cut the Tiger lead to five games, but on July 25 pitcher Joe Sparma put a halt to the Tiger slide by hurling a brilliant one-hitter which the Tigers won 4–1. The next day the Tigers bombed Baltimore 9–0. Horton hit his twenty-fourth and twenty-fifth home runs to lead the Tigers to victory, and things began to look up again.

Batting coach Wally Moses beamed at Horton's performance. He had the greatest confidence in Willie the Wonder.

"This is the year he might break out with forty to forty-five homers," he said. "He is beginning to realize that pitchers are curving him down and away, so he's going to right field with the bat. He's so strong that he can be fooled at the plate, swing late and still put it out of the park."

On August 6 the Tigers won a dramatic seventeen-inning battle from Cleveland, 2–1. It was a typical victory. The Tigers came from behind late in the game to tie and then win it. It marked the twenty-seventh time they had roared from behind as late as the seventh inning, and in nineteen of those games they had managed the winning run in their last time at bat.

With Kaline slowly recovering from his injury and playing in occasional games, the Tigers began to rebuild their league lead again. And Horton continued to enjoy one of his best seasons. On August 22 in Detroit, Horton put on a stellar performance. In the first inning, with McAuliffe and Kaline on base as the result of singles, Horton looped a single into center to drive in a run. Chicago went into the lead, 2–1, in the fourth, but in the sixth Kaline homered and Horton, taking the hint, hit his twenty-ninth of the season. Horton's was the ultimate winning run as the Tigers won 4–2.

Despite the victory, however, it was another tragic game for the Detroit team. During the game, a fight erupted between Dick McAuliffe and Chicago pitcher Tommy John, in which John tore ligaments in his shoulder. McAuliffe was suspended for five days—and immediately the Tigers went into a skid.

The next night, without McAuliffe, who was considered a spark plug on the team, the Tigers lost to New York, 2–1, and then went through a tiring nineteen-inning struggle that ended 3–3 when it was stopped by a curfew. The next day they lost again to New York, 2–1, and their lead over second place Baltimore shrunk to six and a half games.

That wasn't all. The same two teams clashed in a twin bill the next day and New York won them both, 6–5 and 5–4. Now the Tiger lead was down to five games, and just to make it more depressing, Kaline pulled a muscle and was sidelined again.

Despite the Yankees' four straight wins over Detroit, New

York manager Ralph Houk said, "I still think Detroit will win the pennant. They're a good solid club with good pitching."

That's when Mayo Smith went out on a limb. "Houk's right," he said. "We're going to win it. A lot of people want to bury you on what happens in one series."

The Tigers moved to Chicago where they won one game and lost one—and the lead shrunk to four games over Baltimore. But toward the end of August, with the Tigers at their lowest ebb, the team finally got back on the winning track. Horton was one of the prime reasons. In a game against the Angels at Detroit, the Tigers faced their nemesis, George Brunet. The game remained scoreless until the fourth inning, when Willie faced Brunet for the second time in the game. He had fanned the first time, but on this occasion he drilled a Brunet pitch to right field. The ball soared into the seats—a wrong-field home run—to put the Tigers ahead, 1–0.

In the eighth the Tigers were still nursing their slim lead. Dick Tracewski led off the inning with a walk and romped to third when Mickey Stanley rapped a single to center. Willie Horton then slapped another single to left field and drove in the Tigers' second run. That was the ball game—2–0, favor of the Tigers.

After the game Brunet shook his head dolefully. "He's a strong man, that Horton. On his homer, I threw a sinker and got it a little high. You can't get pitches high on Horton anymore. He's a tough hitter."

Willie, himself, didn't know what he hit. When he was told it was a sinker, he said, "No kiddin', is that what it was?"

In the clubhouse after the game Horton ambled to the drinking fountain and downed a pill. A newspaperman noticed it and immediately sensed a story.

"What are you taking, Willie?" he asked.

"Well," said Horton, "for a while I was taking eight pills a day. For the pain."

"Pain? Where are you hurting now?"

"All over," said Willie.

The reporter looked at him suspiciously. There were those among Willie's acquaintances who suspected Horton was a hypochondriac—one who only thinks he's hurting. These people claimed that Horton often ran full-tilt to catch a fly ball, then limped back to his position as if his leg was about to fall off.

"I'm only taking four pills now," Horton went on affably. "You know, when I go home after a game I'm all right for a while. Then all of a sudden I can't walk. So I take a pill."

The conversation drifted back to the home run he had hit, his thirty-first of the season.

"Do you hit certain pitches better than others?" he was asked.

"Naw. I hit 'em all the same," Horton said. "When I'm hitting, I hit any pitcher. When I'm not hitting, I can't see them when they come right down the middle."

"I notice some of the pitchers are brushing you back now," suggested the writer.

"Yeah. But that doesn't bother me. I respect a pitcher when he busts it in on me. Not when he throws at your head—I don't mean that. But when he comes in tight—well, he's just trying to do his job. Take that Seeburn the other night. [He meant Sonny Siebert of Cleveland.] He admitted he was throwing at me. He had me in the dirt eight times in one night. That's baseball, I guess."

As the end of August neared, the Tigers met Baltimore in a three-game series that represented the Orioles' last opportunity to gain ground on the Tigers. Detroit took two of the three games. So, with only a month to go, the Tigers had built an eight-game lead over second place Baltimore, and Detroiters were beginning to talk pennant with more confidence than they had had in twenty-three years. The Tigers had not won a pennant since 1945, but this year looked like the one that would break the dry spell.

That Willie Horton was a major contributor to the Tigers' high standing goes without saying. It was Wonderful Willie's big year. All the things they had been predicting for Horton were coming true in 1968, and his big year was leading the Tigers toward a confrontation with the St. Louis Cardinals in the 1968 World Series.

It had taken Detroiters a little time to believe in the Tigers, because they had been disappointed so often before. But now they were falling in step with the rampaging team. They were convinced that with a month to go and an eight-game lead, the Sock-It-To-'Em Tigers would certainly not blow it.

On September 4 the Tigers played one of their typical games. They were in Oakland and the game was tied, 2–2, in the eighth inning. The first two men for the Tigers were easy outs, and it looked as if the tie might hold up for the rest of the night. But Mickey Stanley walked and Jim Northrup rapped a single to center that moved him to third. Al Kaline then walked and the bases were loaded with Horton ambling to the plate.

Jack Aker was on the mound and he worked with care on the big Detroit slugger. Horton swung and missed the first pitch, and then Aker tried to pitch him low and away. Horton swung and smashed the ball back to the pitchers' mound so fast that Aker had no chance to react. The ball bounced off his glove for a single and Stanley raced home with the lead run. A walk to Freehan forced in another and the Tigers won the game, 4–2.

It was the thirty-fifth time the Tigers had come on to win in the late innings.

The next night the Tigers increased their lead over the field to nine games with an 8–3 win over Minnesota. In that one, Horton hit a home run and a double and drove in five runs to increase his season RBI total to 78.

Sharing the spotlight with Horton was pitcher Denny McLain, who was fashioning a brilliant season for himself. With twenty-eight wins under his belt on September 6, he was on his way to winning thirty games in a season—the first time since 1931 that an American League pitcher had done it.

Everyone around the league was now jumping on the Tiger bandwagon. Bill Rigney, manager of the California Angels, after a defeat by the Tigers in which Horton hit two home runs, was completely candid about the Tigers' chances. "They have the pennant sewed up," he said. "And I think they'll whip the St. Louis Cardinals in the World Series, too."

Horton, himself, was a little more cautious when a reporter said, "It looks as if Detroit is gaining momentum for the World Series."

"Maybe so," Willie said carefully. "I hope we're ready for the Series if it comes. But we haven't won the pennant yet and right now we've got to bear down every game. Everyone around here knows that."

"What about yourself, Willie?" the reporter asked. "Would you like to hit forty homers this year?"

"I'm not really thinking about that," Horton answered honestly. "Nothing's important to me except winning."

Then came September 14 and one of the classic games in Tiger history.

Tiger pitcher Denny McLain was going for his thirtieth win of the season against the Oakland Athletics at Tiger Stadium, and there had been a big publicity buildup for the event. Everyone looked forward to seeing McLain at his best, but as so often happens, Denny was not as sharp a pitcher on his big day as he would have liked. The game was a tense struggle from beginning to end, and when the Tigers came up for their last chance in the bottom of the ninth the score was Oakland 4, Detroit 3.

It looked as if McLain would not get his thirtieth victory that day, because at this point Mayo Smith had to take him out of the lineup for a pinch hitter. This meant that the Tigers would have to stage a winning rally in the last half of the ninth to make the departed McLain a victor.

It was Al Kaline, who had spent the day on the bench, who hit for McLain, and Oakland pitcher Diego Segui, trying to protect his one-run lead, pitched too carefully and walked him. Dick McAuliffe failed to help the situation by popping out, but Mickey Stanley came through with a line single to center field and Kaline raced around to third.

Runners on first and third, one out. There was still hope.

Jim Northrup was now up and the A's pulled in their infield to make a play at the plate if Northrup hit the ball on the ground. Northrup did just that, topping a pitch and dribbling it to first base. Kaline put on a burst of speed and headed for home with the tying run, and Oakland first baseman Danny Cater, trying to nail Kaline at the plate, threw wild over catcher Dave Duncan's head.

The score was now tied, 4-4, with Northrup on first and Stanley on third.

And it was Willie Horton's turn to bat.

A crescendo of cheers went up as Horton stepped up to the plate. Tiger hopes were high now. All it would take to score the winning run from third was a long fly to the outfield.

Nobody was more conscious of this fact than Diego Segui as he wiped perspiration from his brow and got ready to pitch to the muscular Detroit slugger. The Athletics, knowing a long fly would score the winning run, elected to pull in both their infielders and outfielders. The theory was that a long fly would score the man in any case, so the best chance to stop it was to pull in and try to cut off a short hit to the outfield before it dropped in.

Segui went into his stretch, cocked his leg, and buzzed a strike past the stationary Horton. The next pitch cut the outside corner and Horton fouled it off.

Segui was showing no fright over Horton. The next pitch was

in there, too, and Horton fouled it into the dirt. Then, trying to catch the outside corner for the third strike, Segui missed with two pitches.

Ball two, strike two.

Horton tapped the plate gently with the bat, took a few threatening practice swings and waited for the 2–2 pitch. Segui stretched, kicked his leg, threw the ball. It came in waist high and over the plate. Horton swung and felt the shock of ball hitting bat up his arms. The ball took off on a line to left field, passed over the scrambling figure of left fielder Jim Gosger and crashed against the barrier. Stanley came home with the winning run—and Denny McLain had his thirtieth win of the year!

Not only was this a milestone in McLain's career, but it represented the thirty-fifth time in the season that the Tigers had rallied to win from the seventh inning on.

In the clubhouse after the historic game, Horton played down his own contribution to the victory. His thoughts were all on McLain.

"Denny deserves it," he said. "He's a great guy and he's worked hard all year long. Winning thirty games—that's just beautiful!

After this dramatic game there was hardly anything for the Tigers to do that would excite the fans—except to clinch the pennant. This they did on September 17 by whipping the New York Yankees at Tiger Stadium as the Orioles lost. The victory was followed by a rollicking exhibition of enthusiasm as the fans stormed onto the field. The pent-up emotions of twenty-three long years made Tiger Stadium a bedlam.

Only one slightly depressing matter remained. The Tigers would meet the St. Louis Cardinals in the 1968 World Series, and the Cardinals were considered 8 to 5 favorites to take the flag.

Chapter 18

For Willie Horton, the 1968 season had been his best in the majors. He had batted .285, collected 36 home runs and batted in 85, establishing himself as one of the most feared hitters in the game.

After the pennant was clinched, Horton was rested for six days to get over a sinus infection while the Tigers played out their schedule. During this interim Horton returned to Northwestern High School to talk to students, shake hands with old friends and, surprisingly, to take a little batting practice against a high school pitcher on old Diamond No. 1 where Willie had been a star high school player. His old high school coach, Sam Bishop, looked on with pride.

From the steps of the school, with his wife Pat at his side and his daughter, Terri, in his arms, Horton talked to the assembled students.

"I felt sick all week, but today I feel good," he said. "I want to say just one thing. Northwestern High made me a better man in life and taught me to reach my goals. I'll always be here to help my school."

There were cheers of "Sock it to 'em, Willie!" and a banner was raised above the crowd that read: THE TIGERS CAN'T LOSE BECAUSE THEY HAVE A NORTHWESTERN MAN. A few moments later Principal Melvin Chapman drew more cheers when he announced that Horton had promised to dedicate his "first home run" in the Series to Northwestern, and his second to the Northwestern Men's Club.

As the day for the start of the World Series neared, Horton made a statement that "We're ready for the Cardinals. I think we can beat them." Not everyone was in accord with that prediction. The Tigers were underdogs in the World Series. After all, the St. Louis Cardinals were old hands at World Series play, having defeated the Boston Red Sox in 1967. The Tigers had not been in a Series for twenty-three years, and they had a comparatively young team that might well tighten up under the pressure of World Series play.

Besides, manager Mayo Smith had a perplexing problem. He simply had to get the sixteen-year veteran, Al Kaline, into the lineup for the Series. The question was how to do it. The Tigers had three performers in the outfield who had carried the team while Kaline was injured—Northrup, Stanley and Horton. Smith wanted to keep them all in the lineup and still play Kaline. Finally, the Tiger manager took a big gamble. He shifted Stanley to shortstop—a position he had never played—in order to install Kaline in right field. The "experts" immediately went into a swoon.

"He's flipped!" they said. "Imagine putting an untried kid in at short in a World Series! It doesn't make sense—and it won't work."

But Stanley played the last few games of the regular season at shortstop and did fairly well. So when the Tigers took the field at St. Louis' magnificent Busch Stadium for the first game of the World Series, Stanley was at short and the outfield consisted of Northrup, Kaline and Horton.

The first game was expected to be a classic pitchers' battle. Detroit's thirty-one-game winner, Denny McLain, was hooked up in a duel with St. Louis' sterling Bob Gibson, who had six straight World Series victories under his belt. But this time McLain failed to measure up. He was rapped for three runs in the fourth inning and that put the game on ice. Gibson completely baffled the Tigers for the entire game, setting a new World Series strikeout record of seventeen. Willie Horton was a victim twice, and it was he who stood looking dubiously at the plate in the ninth inning as Gibson registered his seventeenth whiff.

Gibson's performance brought nothing but praise from the envious Tigers. And St. Louis fans were quick to point out that "if the Tigers are lucky, they'll face Gibson only twice." The implication was that the Cardinals could wrap up the Series in six games and that Gibson would not have to pitch three times.

And before the second game the odds-makers made St. Louis 14-to-5 favorites in the Series.

But the Tigers got their revenge in the second game. Mickey Lolich was on the mound for the Tigers, and Nelson Briles started for the Cardinals. Having dropped the first game, the Tigers were noticeably tense in the second. Briles retired three batters in a row in the first inning and got the top man in the second. That brought Willie Horton to the plate.

Horton didn't wait. Briles hurled the first pitch plateward and Willie swung. The ball took off in a high arc and dropped into the left field stands at the 386-foot mark. It was the first World Series home run for a Tiger since Hank Greenberg hit two in the 1945 Series. *That one,* thought Willie, *is for Northwestern High.*

Horton's home run sparked the Tigers and dissipated the tension. They went on to score eight runs and defeat the Cardinals, 8–1.

It was in the sixth inning, though, with the Tigers ahead 6–1 that Mayo Smith made a defensive move that caused Willie Horton some personal anguish. Smith moved Stanley back to his natural position in center field, shifted Northrup to left, put Ray Oyler in at short and benched Horton.

Horton discussed the matter with the manager after the game.

"I didn't like being taken out," he said. "I've played out there all year and I'm not too bad a left fielder."

"I had to do it, Willie," insisted Smith. "It's not that you can't cover ground on defense, but there is a difference in throwing. If the same situation arises in another game, I'll have to do the same thing."

Horton reluctantly accepted the explanation. "Anyway, we won," he said, "and that's the important thing."

The Series now shifted to Tiger Stadium, where the Tigers felt they would have the home field advantage. They would be playing three games at home, and if they could win two of them they would be in excellent shape. Of course, they would have to face the remarkable Bob Gibson again—not an appetizing thought.

But things then fell apart for the Tigers. In the third game the Cardinal bats suddenly came to life and hammered Tiger pitching for a 7–3 win. Meantime, the Tigers managed only four hits, and Willie had none.

Needless to say, the Cardinals were delighted. They now had a 2-to-1 edge in the Series, and Bob Gibson would be on the mound for them the next day. If Gibson won, it would give them an almost insurmountable 3-to-1 advantage.

The fourth game was played in a cold drizzle that was almost unfit for baseball. And the bottom fell out again for Detroit. Gibson outpitched Denny McLain again, allowing the Tigers only five hits while his mates bombarded the Detroit pitching staff. The result was a dreary 10–1 defeat for the Tigers that gave the edge in the Series to St. Louis, three games to one.

The Tigers now had an almost impossible task facing them—

they had to win three games in a row from the Cards and, if the Series went seven games, they would have to face the incomparable Gibson in the last contest!

Not only that, but the odds-makers now reported the Tigers were 8-to-1 underdogs.

The fifth game opened as if the Cardinals were determined to put the championship in their hip pockets—fast. They jumped on Mickey Lolich for three runs in the top of the first inning, and Tiger supporters groaned. It looked now as if the Tigers were doomed. They not only had to win three straight games, but they were three runs down in the first inning of the first of those three games!

Meanwhile, Nelson Briles held the Tigers in the palm of his hand. He set them down easily in the first three innings, and when Detroit came to bat in the bottom of the fourth the score was still Cardinals 3, Tigers 0.

Mickey Stanley led off in the fourth, and he caught one of Briles' fast balls and powered it into right field. It bounced off the barrier and before it was returned to the infield, Stanley was perched on third base with a triple. Suddenly the Tiger fans came to life. Kaline was up and, surely, he would deliver. But Al tried to check his swing and tapped a pitch back to the mound. Briles threw him out at first as Stanley held third.

Horton was next up. Willie set himself carefully in the box, took a couple of practice swings, then cocked his bat over his right shoulder. Briles came in with a pitch and Horton swung. It was well tagged—a long belt into deep center field that bounded off the fence. Horton turned second and raced into third with the second triple of the inning—which matched a World Series record. Stanley, of course, scored, and when Jim Northrup singled to right, Horton came home.

Now the score was Cardinals 3, Tigers 2, and the fans began

to remember how often the Tigers had come from behind to win during the season. Could they do it now, in a World Series?

Startled by the sudden Tiger surge, the Cardinals tried to rally in the fifth. Lou Brock, a speedster on the bases, cracked a double off Lolich. Hoolie Javier rapped a single to short left, and Brock, away with the pitch, raced around third and headed for the plate.

Willie Horton, in left, came in fast on the ball. He snapped it up on the second bounce and fired it home. No one in the park thought he had a chance of catching the speedy Brock—but the ball traveled like a bullet into the mitt of catcher Bill Freehan, and Brock was out at the plate.

It was the fielding gem of the day and it stopped a Cardinal rally that might have put the game away for them.

The Tigers threatened in the sixth when they loaded the bases, but they were unable to score. Going into the last of the seventh, the score was still 3–2 favor of the Cardinals.

Don Wert opened the seventh for the Tigers by striking out. That brought up Lolich, a weak hitter. Although he had pitched a good game since the horrible first inning, the fans thought Mayo Smith would take him out for a pinch hitter. When he didn't, the fans became restless. Why let Lolich bat? The Tigers needed a run badly. But Lolich did the unlikely by punching a single to right. That was all for Briles. He trudged off the mound and Joe Hoerner came in. Dick McAuliffe greeted him with a single and Stanley walked. That loaded the bases with one out.

It was Al Kaline who delivered a single to score two runs, and Norm Cash followed with another to make it three runs for the inning. The score was now Detroit 5, St. Louis 3—and that is the way it ended.

Now the Cardinals enjoyed only a one-game lead over the Tigers. But the Series was shifting back to St. Louis for the sixth game and, if necessary, the seventh.

St. Louis fans were sure the Cards would wrap it up in the

sixth game, but the Tigers had other ideas. They scored twice in the second inning, and in the third they went on one of the most remarkable sprees in World Series history, scoring ten runs! It was the first time since 1929 that a team had scored that many runs in a World Series inning. Willie Horton was up twice that inning and walked and singled. He got two hits out of three at-bats for the day, and the Tigers won by the lopsided score of 13–1.

And that brought the Series down to the seventh and last game. The Tigers would have to go up against the formidable Bob Gibson in the deciding contest.

St. Louis fans were now willing to admit that the pesky Tigers had made a fine comeback, but now it would end. There was no question in their minds but that Bob Gibson would stop them in their tracks, just as he had done twice before. Besides, the Cardinal batters were bound to get to Mickey Lolich, the Tiger pitcher. After all, he was pitching with only two days' rest.

The game was one of the most tense in World Series play. Both pitchers were superb. For six nail-biting innings the two teams battled each other. Neither was able to score. It was a knock-down, drag-out scoreless ball game.

The top of the seventh inning opened as dismally for the Tigers as the previous six. Mickey Stanley was called out on strikes and Al Kaline bounced an easy ground ball to third base. Two out, nobody on.

But then came the fireworks. Norm Cash singled sharply to right. Willie Horton was up and he clobbered one of the incomparable Gibson's pitches into left field for a single. Jim Northrup then delivered the key blow—a long triple over Curt Flood's head in center field that scored both Tiger runners. When Bill Freehan smashed a double to left, the Tigers had three runs.

The Tigers had the great Bob Gibson on the ropes!

Now the St. Louis fans were strangely silent. They watched

as the Tigers scored one more run in the top of the ninth. In the Cardinal half of the ninth they also scored one run, but the final score was Detroit 4, St. Louis 1!

The Detroit Tigers, for the first time in twenty-three years, had won a World Series! And they had done it the hard way, coming from behind with three straight victories!

Both the Detroit clubhouse and the city of Detroit went wild after the victory. In the clubhouse after the game there was complete chaos. General manager Jim Campbell, owner John Fetzer, manager Mayo Smith and all the Tigers were in an uproarious mood. Champagne corks popped and players squirted the bubbly liquid at each other. Lolich stood in a corner and emptied a bottle of champagne over his own head. Some of the players did a wild dance around the room, others shouted, and some of them even cried.

Willie Horton, who had come such a long way from the ghettos of Detroit to a spot with the World Champion Tigers, was saying little, but his face was wreathed with smiles.

"It's just like Christmas came early," he said to anyone who would listen. "Man, oh, man—I looked up there on top of the left field roof in the seventh inning when we got our runs, and there was Rudolph the Rednosed Reindeer!" He chuckled at his own description of his happiness. "Man, oh, man!" he said again. "I've never been this happy in my life. Never! Never! Never!"

Back in Detroit the city was already in a gigantic celebration. Ticker tape and torn-up phonebooks were tossed out of office buildings in the downtown area, and happy people who had waited twenty-three years for a pennant left their work to mingle in the streets. Thousands raced out to the airport to meet the Tiger plane when it came in—so many that they blocked the runways and the Tigers had to land elsewhere.

Probably the most significant fact of all was that the celebration knew no race, creed or color. The year before, the city of Detroit had been rocked by riots and violence; this year it was rocked again by a peaceful celebration in which all forgot their differences.

Sociologists later said that this was the biggest contribution the Tigers had made to Detroit.

Chapter 19

In 1969 a major change was made in the structure of professional baseball. It was the first year of divisional play. Both the American and National Leagues were split into divisions of East and West, with the 162-game schedule determining only the divisional champions. A five-game playoff between the Eastern and Western winners at the end of the season was introduced to determine the two teams that would face each other in the World Series.

The Detroit Tigers found themselves in the Eastern division of the American League, along with the Boston Red Sox, Baltimore Orioles, New York Yankees, Cleveland Indians and Washington Senators.

The year 1969 also saw the first player strike in history. In an effort to force concessions from baseball management on their pension program, organized ballplayers refused to show up for spring training in Florida. The issue was not settled until the regulars had lost about ten days of training in Florida camps.

But the World Champion Detroit Tigers fared well when they got down to settling their contracts for 1969. All of them received generous raises in salary as a reward for their fine season and their victory over the St. Louis Cardinals.

During the winter months Willie Horton was a busy man. He had his name legally changed from William Wattison Horton to Willie Horton because "everything I'm now in is in the name of Willie, so there won't be any complications." He busied himself working for increased school millage because "we intend to stay in Detroit and make our home here, so the least we can do for our fine Detroit youngsters is to give them a boost up the ladder of success as coach Sam Bishop and the teachers at Northwestern High did for me." He also joined the Harlem Globetrotters, making public appearances and occasionally playing basketball for a few minutes; and when he wasn't doing that he was working on his batting stroke, taking his cuts at balls thrown by a pitching machine in a local gymnasium. "I want to be in shape in case the pension fight interferes with our spring training," he said.

On salary negotiations, Horton held out and was the last man on the Tiger team to sign—for $60,000. Then he went to work with his usual dedication at Lakeland, Florida.

Only one thing happened to mar Willie's spring training grind. His wife and children were again unable to find accommodations near the Tiger training camp, and finally, in frustration, Patricia took the children home to Detroit. Horton was bitter about it.

"I didn't have any choice but to send my wife and children home," he said. "The only houses they showed us down here you wouldn't take a dog into. I wouldn't want my family in places like that."

Members of the Tigers were quartered at the Holiday Inn, and there were no problems there, but a motel room was not adequate for a player whose family was with him—and Horton's family could not find a house to rent in all of Lakeland.

In addition, Horton ran into stiff trouble on the field. In the first ten games of the Grapefruit season, he collected only four hits. But as the spring training games drew to an end, Horton was again tagging the ball and looking forward to a good year.

The Tigers opened the 1969 season at home against the Cleveland Indians, and they presented the same lineup that had taken the St. Louis Cardinals apart so handily in the World Series. The infield had Dick McAuliffe at second base, Mickey Stanley at short, Norm Cash at first, Don Wert at third and Bill Freehan behind the bat. The outfield consisted of Al Kaline in right, Jim Northrup in center and Willie Horton in left. The opening day pitcher was Denny McLain, who held the Indians to three hits as the Tigers won, 6–2.

Willie Horton had 1-for-5 in the first game, and in the second he hit 2-for-4, including his first home run. The Tigers won that one 12–3.

But then frustration set in. By April 17 the Tigers were just over .500 with seven wins and six losses. They struggled for another week, and on April 30 they had ten wins and nine losses.

The Tigers, who had burned up the league the year before and were expected to win it all again in 1969, found it difficult to put together a winning streak. Puzzled and uncertain of themselves, they began to press—and by the middle of May they found themselves in fourth place with fourteen wins and sixteen losses, six and a half games behind the fast-moving first place Baltimore Orioles.

Personally, Willie Horton was also having a difficult time. He was beset with personal problems, the nature of which he divulged to no one. On the field, he was impotent. Something was wrong with his hitting and he didn't know what. He was swinging at bad pitches, not getting his usual power into his hits, and he was continually leaving runners stranded on the bases—so many of them that the fans not only noticed it but grew vocal about it.

On May 14, in a game with the Chicago White Sox at Tiger Stadium, Willie heard the boos of the home crowd for the first time in his career. A favorite at the ball park, Horton had heard only scattered boos on rare occasions—but on this night they were loud and insistent.

They started in the third inning when Horton came to bat with two men on and bounced into a force play to end the inning. In the sixth he let a single to left field slip past him and the boos increased. And they descended upon his bowed head as he went back to the dugout after having struck out in the Tiger half of the sixth.

In the clubhouse after the Tiger defeat, Horton had a worried look on his face.

"I don't know why they're on me," he said solemnly. "I know I'm not going well, but I'm doing my best. That's all that counts for me. If those fans weren't behind us, they wouldn't be out here. That's the way I have to figure it."

Mayo Smith was worried by the reaction of the fans, too. He knew what was happening. When a team flounders badly, the crowd always gets on the big man, using him as a target for their wrath. The crowd expected much of Willie, and when he failed consistently to come through, he became their target for abuse.

"Horton's a sensitive young man," said Smith with concern. "The booing could bother him."

The next night the Tigers hooked up with Chicago again, and Horton went out on the field determined to change the boos to cheers. He was hitting only .213, with four home runs, and he had not hit a homer in two and a half weeks. He was due for a change.

But the Tigers found themselves up against a skillful Tommy John, who was stingy with the hits, and Horton's experience was disastrous.

Up for the first time in the second inning, Horton grounded out to Luis Aparicio at short. The boos began to rumble in the stands. In the fourth inning, with two men out and Al Kaline on base, Horton struck out—and the boos increased. In the sixth Norm Cash was on base and Willie struck out again. The boos cascaded down.

Horton went to his position in left field with his mind a jumble. True, he wasn't producing, but he was not the only one. Mickey Stanley had just gone through an 0-for-20 dry spell, and Don Wert was hitting only .106. But the fans were taking out their disappointment on Willie Horton because they expected so much more of their hero.

Fiery resentment swept through Willie's mind as he returned to the dugout after the seventh inning. He did not stop at the bench. Furiously, he stormed through the dugout and into the clubhouse—and the Tigers looked at each other in stunned amazement. Mickey Stanley and pitching coach Johnny Sain finally went after him, and in the deserted clubhouse they found an angry Horton tossing off his uniform and getting dressed.

"Come on back, Willie," Stanley said. "You can't walk out in the middle of the game."

Sain pleaded with the furious Horton, but Willie would not listen. At last Sain went back to the dugout and approached Mayo Smith.

"Willie Horton is leaving," he said.

Smith stared at Sain unbelievingly. The Tigers went on to win the game, 2–1, but the victory was hollow. The Tiger clubhouse after the game was silent.

Willie Horton had disappeared.

The Tigers had no recourse but to suspend Willie without pay until he returned to the club. Horton, meantime, dropped from sight, was unavailable to newspaper reporters, and did not show up for the flight of the team to Minnesota for the next day's game.

While the Tigers prepared to meet the Twins without Horton's aid, friends of Willie's tried to help him. Freddy Snowden, assistant basketball coach at the University of Michigan, was one of them. Damon Keith, onetime guardian for Willie, flew in from New York to talk to him. Somehow the word got out that Willie Horton wanted to be traded, and Snowden finally talked by phone to newspaper reporters.

"Willie wants me to say this," he said. "He does not want to be traded and never has made such a statement. He's said many times that Detroit fans are the best in the world. It's not the boos that caused him to walk out. There are personal things involved that he's trying to work out."

Willie Horton missed the Minnesota series, and when the Tigers came back to Detroit, Horton met with general manager Jim Campbell. He agreed to return to the team the next day when they were scheduled to meet the White Sox in Chicago. This was good news, especially for the children—for newspaper offices were swamped with calls from young fans who wanted to know when Willie would return. He was a favorite player who was having a bad season, and the adult fans had booed. The kids had never deserted him.

Horton was not unaware of that loyalty. After his agreement with Campbell, he said, "I made a big mistake and I'm sorry. Now I just hope the kids, the fans and the ballplayers forgive me."

Playing in Chicago, Willie knew there were few Detroit fans in the ball park to either harass or cheer him. But thousands of Detroiters were listening to the broadcast of the game on radio, and Horton didn't want to let them down. He desperately needed their forgiveness, and if ever he wanted to do well in a game it was now.

Horton received a chance to redeem himself in the very first inning. The left-handed Tommy John was on the mound for the White Sox and, with one out, he got into trouble. Dick McAuliffe and Al Kaline both singled, and then John walked Norm Cash. That loaded the bases and Horton walked up to bat.

Horton felt a little nervousness seep through him as he took his position at the plate, but it subsided as he concentrated on the pitcher. Tommy John peered in for his sign, got it, glanced at the eager runners dancing off the bases and fired a strike past the stationary Horton. Willie stepped out, got back in, waved his bat menacingly and waited for the next pitch. John came in with a hopping fast ball and Willie ripped a line drive to center field. It carried over outfielder Ken Berry's head and slammed against the barrier 415 feet away. One foot higher and it would have gone in for a grand slam home run. Instead, Horton pulled up at second with a double that scored both McAuliffe and Kaline.

That was dramatic enough, but there was more. In the sixth inning he smashed an infield hit to third that drove in Kaline, his third RBI of the game. Altogether, the Tigers scored seven, winning the game 7–6.

A couple of days later the Tigers were back home to play the California Angels, and Horton was to play his first game before the home crowd since walking out on the team. Despite his heroics in Chicago, there was much conjecture about how the home fans would greet him. Horton, himself, was not sure.

But when he walked out on the field to take batting practice, his concern evaporated. His personal fans—those who always gathered in the left field seats—were pouring in long before the game began, and there was boisterous applause as Horton stepped into the batting cage for the first time. A sign was unfurled in the left field seats that read, "Welcome Home, Willie!" The sign and the noisy crowd sent a chill through Horton. The best fans in the world, he had called them—and they were.

Horton responded to the ovation by slapping four balls into the left field seats for the customers. On his second turn in the batting cage he drilled two more into the seats, and followed with another two in his third appearance. And when he ran out to his position for the start of the game, the fans rose to their feet and cheered loudly.

But the real indication of the fans' support came when Horton walked to the plate to lead off in the second inning. The crowd in the left field seats began smashing empty seats up and down and cheering widely. Then the entire park exploded with noisy cheering. There were a few isolated boos, but the ovation drowned them out.

Andy Messersmith was pitching for the Angels, and Horton responded to the support by slapping a single to left field. It was his only hit of the night, but it brought down the house.

The Tigers came from a 3–0 deficit to win the game, 6–3, and when it was over Horton was feeling good again.

"The way those fans acted was wonderful," he said. "Just beautiful. I want them to know I didn't desert them."

Encouraged, Willie's hitting improved for a brief period after his return to the lineup. But it fell off abruptly again. He found himself in a deep and mysterious slump, and for a while the rest of the team carried him. In the last two weeks of May the Tigers won thirteen out of sixteen games, but were unable to gain on the rampaging Baltimore Orioles. On that date the Tigers trailed the Orioles by six and a half games.

Horton worried about his personal batting slump. So did manager Mayo Smith. Finally, Smith made a move.

"I'm going to play you against left-handers only for a while," he told Willie. "Gates Brown will play when a right-hander is on the hill. We'll see what happens."

What happened was that Gates Brown took sick and went into the hospital and Willie stayed in left field—and continued to slump. Some of the boos continued as he floundered at the plate, but there were loyal fans who cheered him too.

"I don't understand the booing," he said wearily. "I work

hard at everything I do. Maybe that's what's the matter. Trying too hard."

On June 15 the Tigers attempted to strengthen their position in the American League race by acquiring the services of Tom Tresh from the New York Yankees in exchange for outfielder Ron Woods. Although the move strengthened the team on paper, it did little toward overtaking the racing Baltimore Orioles. By the third week in June the Tigers were in third place, trailing the Orioles by eleven games!

The pennant was beginning to look a long way off!

On June 22 Willie Horton had the crowd on its feet with one of his rare performances. The Tigers were playing the Washington Senators at Tiger Stadium. In the first inning the Tigers scored a run and had men on second and third with two out. Willie Horton, who had been dropped to sixth in the batting order, was up, but Washington manager Ted Williams wasn't about to gamble on even a slumping Horton. He ordered pitcher Jim Shellenback to walk him, and the strategy worked when Jim Northrup ended the inning with a fly ball.

Washington held a 2–1 lead when Horton came to bat for the second time in the fourth inning. This time he caught a Shellenback fast ball squarely and sent it screaming into the left field stands for a game-tying home run. In the fifth he came to bat with Norm Cash on second and drilled a single to left field that drove Cash home. Then came the critical seventh inning.

The two teams were deadlocked, 5–5, and Washington now had Bob Humphreys on the mound. Al Kaline greeted him with a single, and Cash followed with a blooper over shortstop. That finished Humphreys, and Casey Cox came in for the Senators. Ike Brown, replacing an injured and slumping Don Wert at third base, laid down a bunt single and the bases were loaded.

Willie Horton walked slowly to the plate, placed himself in the batter's box with infinite care and leveled his bat at the Washington pitcher. Cox went into his stretch and came in with the first pitch, and Willie drove it out again—clear out of the park, in fact, for the second grand slam homer of his career. The tremendous blast won the game for the Tigers, 9–5. Horton had driven in six of the runs.

"You haven't been hitting well lately," said a reporter in the clubhouse. "How'd it feel?"

"It felt fine. But the important thing is that we won."

"Do you think this will give you a lift?"

Willie grinned. "I hope so. I just can't continue hitting bad forever."

But on June 26 Willie suffered another bad break. In a game with Baltimore he pulled a leg muscle and sat on the bench for the next three weeks. Sitting out a game always hurt Willie. He would remain on the bench, fidgeting, for five or six innings, and then he could no longer tolerate the inactivity. For the last few innings he would be on his feet, pacing the dugout nervously.

The pulled muscle slowly healed and Willie returned to the lineup on July 17. The Tigers were playing the Senators in Washington that night, and the two teams were locked in a scoreless tie when the eighth inning came around. Willie strode to the plate in that inning and, with the bases loaded, lashed a ringing double against the wall in left center to bring home all three runners. It won the game for the Tigers, 3–0.

The next night Willie won another game with one swing of his bat. In the first inning of a game against Washington, with two men on, Willie hit one of Casey Cox's pitches into the left field stands for a three-run homer. The Tigers won the game 3–1.

The following night he hit a two-run homer to pin down a 4–0 victory over the Cleveland Indians, and also had eleven putouts in left field to tie an American League record.

"Man," he said, beaming, "when things are going right for you, this is a beautiful game!"

But it is a tough job bringing your batting average up late in the season, and Willie's rose with point-by-point reluctance as things began to improve for him. Suddenly, he was the right man in the right place at the right time again—a situation that had eluded him all season. On August 3 he found himself once more in the right spot at a critical moment.

The Tigers were at home against the Chicago White Sox, and the two teams were tied at two runs apiece when the Tigers came up to bat in the last of the ninth inning.

Dan Osinski was pitching for the White Sox, and Mickey Stanley beat out an infield hit to open the inning. Tom Tresh forced him at second, but Al Kaline hit one up the middle and Chicago's second baseman, Bobby Knoop, booted the ball. Norm Cash then walked to fill the bases.

Willie Horton lumbered to the plate to face Osinski. The Sox pitcher peered in for the sign, stretched and fired the ball. Horton swung, feeling the satisfactory tingle of contact up his arms. On his way to first base, Willie didn't bother to look up. He knew the ball was gone—high in the upper deck in left field for a grand slammer that won the game, 6–2.

As the month of August progressed, Willie progressed with it. The hits were falling in for him now and the team was winning, and by the end of August the Tigers were in second place, six games ahead of the third place Boston Red Sox. Baltimore, however, was out of sight, leading the Tigers by twelve and a half games. They were doing everything right, as the Tigers had the year before, and no matter how well the Tigers played there was no chance to catch them.

Personally, Willie Horton's batting average had now climbed to .255. "But I want to get it higher than that," he said.

Late in August, Horton's bat really began to spank out a merry tune. He opened an amazing bombardment on a Friday night in Seattle by hitting a home run. On Saturday he hit another. On Sunday he hit two homers, and on Monday two more. On Tuesday he failed to get one, but on Wednesday he belted another. That made it seven home runs in six days, along with four other hits, and gave him 14 RBIs to lift his total to 70 for the season. His home run production, which had sagged so noticeably early in the season, now stood at a respectable 21, and his batting average had climbed painfully but steadily to .260.

When a reporter wanted to know how Willie accounted for his sudden splash of power hitting, Horton grinned. "I don't know what's doing it, but whatever it is, I'll take it. It's about time things were opening up for me."

Willie Horton's bat continued to boom during the month of September. But the Tigers, as a team, sagged. When the month began the Tigers had what looked like a safe six-game lead over the Boston Red Sox in the fight for second place. But the Tigers came up flat, at one point losing seven out of eight games, while Boston won a bundle of them to tie the Tigers for second place. On September 26, with only five games left to play, each team had 86 wins and 71 losses.

But a well-pitched game by Denny McLain put the Tigers one game up on the Red Sox and when the season ended the Tigers had managed to grab second place with 90 wins and 72 losses—three games ahead of the third place Red Sox. Baltimore led the second place Tigers, though, by nineteen games.

Despite a slow start and a rash of troubles throughout the year, Horton had rescued himself from a mediocre season by a persistence that permitted him to finish with a good statistical year. He finished with a batting average of .262, and he had 28 home runs and 91 RBIs to his credit.

There is no doubt that the name of Willie Horton will be a big one in major league baseball for some time to come. With only five full seasons in the majors, he has already established himself as one of the fine right-handed power hitters of the game. Big and strong, he still has many years to go—a fact that inspired one pitcher to remark that "it almost makes a guy want to retire from the league."

But whatever stature Willie Horton achieves in baseball as the years go by, he will never forget his humble beginnings. He has an inherent love of, and sympathy for, young boys born of poor parents who face a struggle in life. Long after Horton hangs up his spikes for the last time, he will be working with boys, helping them to achieve some success in their lives. Willie is a sensitive person who remembers the people who helped him during his own early difficult days, and he will help others by giving generously of himself.

That's the kind of man Willie Horton is.

WILLIE HORTON

Bats right, throws right
Outfielder
Weight: 195
Height: 5'10"

Year	Club	G	AB	R	H	2b	3b	HR	RBI	BB	SO	BA	E	FA
1962	Duluth	123	441	68	130	20	4	15	72	49	46	.295	10	.949
1963	Syracuse	21	78	12	17	2	1	2	8	7	7	.218	1	.977
	Knoxville	118	442	77	147	20	9	14	70	38	55	.333	7	.964
	Detroit	15	43	6	14	2	1	1	4	0	8	.326	0	1.000
1964	Detroit	25	80	6	13	1	3	1	10	11	20	.163	2	.943
	Syracuse	135	490	73	141	16	9	28	99	44	68	.288	10	.964
1965	Detroit	143	512	69	140	20	2	29	104	48	101	.273	3	.989
1966	Detroit	146	526	72	138	22	6	27	100	44	103	.262	5	.979
1967	Detroit	122	401	47	110	20	3	19	67	36	80	.274	5	.971
1968	Detroit	143	512	68	146	20	2	36	85	49	110	.285	6	.973
1969	Detroit	141	508	66	133	17	1	28	91	65	93	.262	8	.972
Major League Totals		735	2582	334	694	102	18	141	461	253	515	.278	29	.974

About the Author

Hal Butler was born in St. Louis, Missouri, but moved to Detroit, Michigan, as a child and has spent most of his life there. Educated in the public schools, he got his first writing experience as a reporter for his high school newspaper.

Always too much of a lightweight to actively participate in major sports, he nevertheless played most sports as a youngster and has kept close to the sport scene during his adult life. His writing career has been one of great variety for the past twenty years, including sport and detective fiction, as well as nonfiction on sports, travel, history, adventure, automobiles and general subjects. Mr. Butler's stories have appeared in *Saturday Evening Post, Coronet, Pageant, Sport, True, American Mercury* and several foreign publications.

At the present time he serves as managing editor on the *Ford Times*, a national travel magazine published by the Ford Motor Company. He and his family live in Southfield, a suburb of Detroit, and commute during the summer months to a log cabin in northwestern Michigan. Other than writing, Mr. Butler's favorite avocation is travel, and he has visited most of the continental United States, Hawaii, Europe, Mexico, Canada and the Caribbean.